MATH Trailblazers®

A BALANCED MATHEMATICS PROGRAM INTEGRATING SCIENCE AND LANGUAGE ARTS

Student Guide

Book 2

THIRD EDITION

KENDALL/HUNT PUBLISHING COMPANY
4050 Westmark Drive   Dubuque, Iowa 52002

A TIMS® Curriculum
University of Illinois at Chicago

MATH TRAILBLAZERS®

Dedication

This book is dedicated to
the children and teachers who
let us see the magic in their classrooms
and to our families who wholeheartedly
supported us while we searched for
ways to make it happen.

The TIMS Project

UIC The University of Illinois
at Chicago

The original edition was based on work supported by the National Science Foundation under grant No. MDR 9050226 and the University of Illinois at Chicago. Any opinions, findings, and conclusions or recommendations expressed in this publication are those of the authors and do not necessarily reflect the views of the granting agencies.

Acknowledgments

Teaching Integrated Mathematics and Science (TIMS) Project Directors
Philip Wagreich, Principal Investigator
Joan L. Bieler
Howard Goldberg (emeritus)
Catherine Randall Kelso

Principal Investigators

First Edition	Philip Wagreich
	Howard Goldberg

Directors

Third Edition	Joan L. Bieler
Second Edition	Catherine Randall Kelso

Senior Curriculum Developers

First Edition	Janet Simpson Beissinger	Carol Inzerillo
	Joan L. Bieler	Andy Isaacs
	Astrida Cirulis	Catherine Randall Kelso
	Marty Gartzman	Leona Peters
	Howard Goldberg	Philip Wagreich

Curriculum Developers

Third Edition	Janet Simpson Beissinger	Philip Wagreich
Second Edition	Lindy M. Chambers-Boucher	Jennifer Mundt Leimberer
	Elizabeth Colligan	Georganne E. Marsh
	Marty Gartzman	Leona Peters
	Carol Inzerillo	Philip Wagreich
	Catherine Randall Kelso	
First Edition	Janice C. Banasiak	Jenny Knight
	Lynne Beauprez	Sandy Niemiera
	Andy Carter	Janice Ozima
	Lindy M. Chambers-Boucher	Polly Tangora
	Kathryn Chval	Paul Trafton
	Diane Czerwinski	

Illustrator

	Kris Dresen

Editorial and Production Staff

Third Edition	Kathleen R. Anderson	Anne Roby
	Lindy M. Chambers-Boucher	
Second Edition	Kathleen R. Anderson	Georganne E. Marsh
	Ai-Ai C. Cojuangco	Cosmina Menghes
	Andrada Costoiu	Anne Roby
	Erika Larson	
First Edition	Glenda L. Genio-Terrado	Sarah Nelson
	Mini Joseph	Biruté Petrauskas
	Lynelle Morgenthaler	

Acknowledgments

TIMS Professional Developers

Barbara Crum	Cheryl Kneubuhler
Catherine Ditto	Lisa Mackey
Pamela Guyton	Linda Miceli

TIMS Director of Media Services

Henrique Cirne-Lima

TIMS Research Staff

Stacy Brown	Catherine Ditto
Reality Canty	Catherine Randall Kelso

TIMS Administrative Staff

Eve Ali Boles	Enrique Puente
Kathleen R. Anderson	Alice VanSlyke
Nida Khan	

Research Consultant

First Edition   Andy Isaacs

Mathematics Education Consultant

First Edition   Paul Trafton

National Advisory Committee

First Edition

Carl Berger	Mary Lindquist
Tom Berger	Eugene Maier
Hugh Burkhardt	Lourdes Monteagudo
Donald Chambers	Elizabeth Phillips
Naomi Fisher	Thomas Post
Glenda Lappan	

TIMS Project Staff

Table of Contents

Additional student pages may be found in the *Adventure Book* or the *Unit Resource Guide.*

Table of Contents

Additional student pages may be found in the *Adventure Book* or the *Unit Resource Guide.*

Letter to Parents

Dear Parents,

Math Trailblazers® is based on the ideas that mathematics is best learned through solving many different kinds of problems and that all children deserve a challenging mathematics curriculum. The program provides a careful balance of concepts and skills. Traditional arithmetic skills and procedures are covered through their repeated use in problems and through distributed practice. *Math Trailblazers,* however, offers much more. Students using this program will become proficient problem solvers, will know when and how to apply the mathematics they have learned, and will be able to clearly communicate their mathematical knowledge. Computation, measurement, geometry, data collection and analysis, estimation, graphing, patterns and relationships, mental arithmetic, and simple algebraic ideas are all an integral part of the curriculum. They will see connections between the mathematics learned in school and the mathematics used in everyday life. And, they will enjoy and value the work they do in mathematics.

The *Student Guide* is only one component of *Math Trailblazers.* Additional material and lessons are contained in the *Adventure Book* and in the teacher's *Unit Resource Guides.* If you have questions about the program, we encourage you to speak with your child's teacher.

This curriculum was built around national recommendations for improving mathematics instruction in American schools and the research that supported those recommendations. The first edition was extensively tested with thousands of children in dozens of classrooms over five years of development. In preparing the second and third editions, we have benefited from the comments and suggestions of hundreds of teachers and children who have used the curriculum. *Math Trailblazers* reflects our view of a complete and well-balanced mathematics program that will prepare children for the 21st century—a world in which mathematical skills will be important in most occupations and mathematical reasoning will be essential for acting as an informed citizen in a democratic society. We hope that you enjoy this exciting approach to learning mathematics and that you watch your child's mathematical abilities grow throughout the year.

Philip Wagreich

Philip Wagreich
Professor, Department of Mathematics, Statistics, and Computer Science
Director, Institute for Mathematics and Science Education
Teaching Integrated Mathematics and Science (TIMS) Project
University of Illinois at Chicago

Unit 11

Ways of Subtracting Larger Numbers

	Student Guide	Adventure Book	Unit Resource Guide*
Lesson 1			
Subtraction with Triangle Flash Cards	●		
Lesson 2			
Subtraction Seminar	●		
Lesson 3			
Is It Reasonable?	●		
Lesson 4			
Base-Ten Subtraction	●		
Lesson 5			
Paper-and-Pencil Subtraction	●		
Lesson 6			
Snack Shop Addition and Subtraction	●		

Unit Resource Guide pages are from the teacher materials.

Triangle Flash Cards: Group A Subtraction Facts

- Cut out the flash cards. To practice a subtraction fact, cover the number in the circle. Subtract the two uncovered numbers.

- Divide the cards into three piles: those facts you know and can answer quickly, those you can figure out with a strategy, and those you need to learn.

- Make a list of the facts in the last two piles. These are the facts you need to study.

- Go through all the cards again. This time cover the number in the square.

- Sort the cards into three piles again. Add the facts in the last two piles to your list that you need to study.

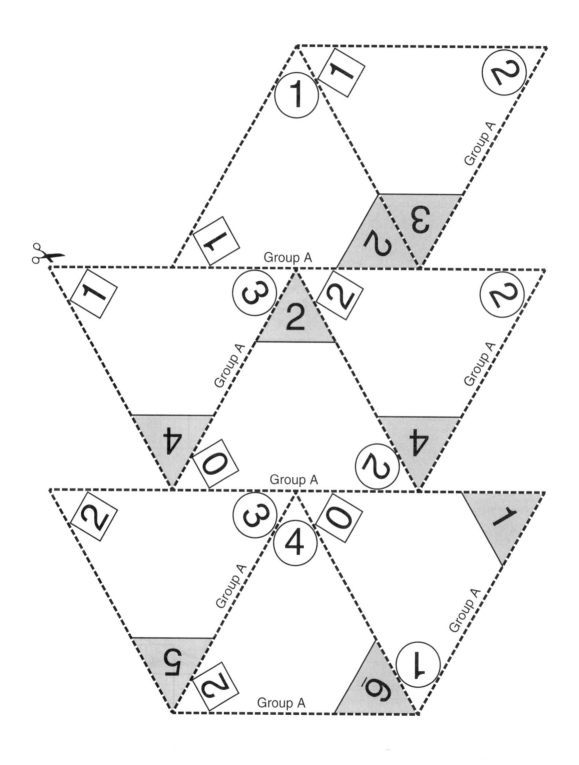

Subtraction with Triangle Flash Cards

Name _____ Date _____

Triangle Flash Cards: Note Home

Dear Family Member:

Your child is beginning a systematic study of the subtraction facts. He or she will study a small group of facts at a time using *Triangle Flash Cards*. These are the same *Triangle Flash Cards* that your child used to practice the addition facts. They are used slightly differently when practicing the subtraction facts.

- Choose a card and cover the corner with the square. Ask your child to subtract the two uncovered numbers.

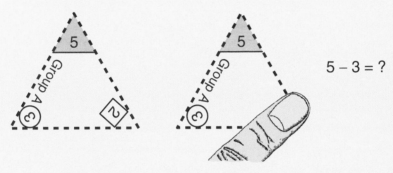

$$5 - 3 = ?$$

- As you work through the cards, divide them into three piles: those facts your child knows and can answer quickly, those your child can figure out with a strategy, and those your child needs to learn.

- Have your child make a list of the facts in the last two piles for further practice.

- Go through the cards again, this time covering the corner with the circle. Separate the cards again into three piles, and make a list of those cards in the last two piles.

- Discuss strategies that are useful for learning these facts.

- Practice the last two piles a second time.

- Help your child study these facts for a few minutes each day.

Thank you.

Name _____ Date _____

More Thinking about Subtraction

Complete the following sentences. Show your thinking below each phrase.

1.

I know that my change is _____ ¢ because

2.

The soup costs _____ ¢ more than the noodles.
I know this because

3.

I need _____ more cents to buy the juice. I know this because

Name _____ Date _____

At the Playground

Dear Family Member:

Our class is working on different ways to solve subtraction problems.
Encourage your child to tell all the different ways that he or she is able
to solve each of the problems below.

Thank you for your cooperation.

Solve the problems in the spaces below. Describe how you solved each problem.

There are 60 children on the playground: 14 are on the swings;
23 are jumping rope; the rest are playing tag. Thirty-three of the
children are boys.

1. How many of the children on the playground are girls?

2. How many children are not jumping rope?

3. How many children are playing tag?

4. In the evening, 47 children went home for dinner. How many children were left on the playground?

Which Answer Makes Sense?

Look at each problem. Decide which number is the best estimate of the correct answer. Explain why you think so in the space below the problem.

1. $\begin{array}{r} 60 \\ -27 \\ \hline \end{array}$ 45   30   50

2. $\begin{array}{r} 50 \\ -18 \\ \hline \end{array}$ 30   40   15

3. $\begin{array}{r} 50 \\ +22 \\ \hline \end{array}$ 30   70   20

4. $\begin{array}{r} 94 \\ -38 \\ \hline \end{array}$ 50   40   75

5. $\begin{array}{r} 71 \\ -34 \\ \hline \end{array}$ 40   50   60

Base-Ten Subtraction

Estimate the answer. Then show how to do the problem with base-ten pieces and one other way.

1. What is 78 – 25? The answer will be between _____ and _____.

with base-ten pieces	another way

2. What is 84 – 55? The answer will be between _____ and _____.

with base-ten pieces	another way

3. The difference will be between _____ and _____.

$$\begin{array}{r} 55 \\ -\,29 \\ \hline \end{array}$$

with base-ten pieces	another way

4. The difference will be between _____ and _____.

$$\begin{array}{r} 60 \\ -\,32 \\ \hline \end{array}$$

with base-ten pieces	another way

Ways to Subtract

Estimate the answer. Then solve the problem. Show how to do the problem with base-ten pieces and one other way.

1. The difference will be between _____ and _____.

$$
\begin{array}{r}
41 \\
-\,29 \\
\hline
\end{array}
$$

with base-ten pieces	another way

2. The difference will be between _____ and _____.

$$
\begin{array}{r}
63 \\
-\,27 \\
\hline
\end{array}
$$

with base-ten pieces	another way

Difference War

Players

This is a game for two or more players.

Materials

- digit cards or regular playing cards
- paper
- pencil

(If you use the regular playing cards, use only the 1–9 cards. Use the ace for one.)

Rules

1. Deal out four cards to each player.
2. Each player makes a subtraction problem with the four cards.
3. Each player solves his or her subtraction problem.
4. The player whose answer is the smallest takes everyone's cards and puts them aside.
5. Deal four more cards to each player and make up more problems. Keep playing until the cards are gone.
6. When all the cards are gone, the player who has collected the most cards wins.

Play several games. Then, write about what happened. Tell how you think you can win.

_____

_____

_____

Name _____ Date _____

More Baseball Cards

Solve the following problems. Draw a picture or write to explain your thinking.

1. Jeremiah has 56 White Sox baseball cards. Jordan has 28. How many more cards does Jeremiah have than Jordan?

2. Jeremiah's mom started collecting baseball cards when she was 8 years old. She is now 44. How many years has she collected cards?

3. Jordan had 34 Cardinal cards. He sold 18 to a friend. How many Cardinal cards does he have left?

4. Jeremiah has 26 Yankee cards, 36 Red Sox cards, and 19 Cardinal cards in his drawer. How many cards are in his drawer?

5.	50 − 32	6.	73 − 42	7.	25 + 48	8.	61 − 38

Many Ways to Find the Answer

Solve the problem three different ways.

Problem

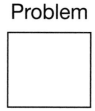

1. First way:

2. Second way:

3. Third way:

Shooting Star Snack Shop
Children's Menu

Food

Pizza Slice.................................... 79¢

Taco.. 59¢

Grilled Cheese Sandwich............. 89¢

Turkey Sandwich......................... 99¢

Peanut Butter and Crackers........ 49¢

Bagel... 29¢

Potato Chips................................ 25¢

Pretzels....................................... 25¢

Brownie....................................... 35¢

Fruit Salad Cup........................... 65¢

Carrot Sticks............................... 29¢

Chicken Noodle Soup.................. 55¢

Chili... 75¢

Drinks	Small	Medium	Large
Milk......................	25¢	40¢	55¢
Lemonade..................	39¢	55¢	79¢
Orange Juice................	55¢	70¢	85¢
Hot Chocolate..............	59¢	75¢	99¢

Snack Shop Bills 2

You have $1.75. Do you have enough money to buy the items listed below?	You have 40¢. Do you have enough money to buy the items listed below?
Estimate: yes _____ no _____	**Estimate:** yes _____ no _____
Actual:	**Actual:**
Peanut Butter and Crackers _____	Bagel _____
Chicken Noodle Soup _____	Pretzels _____
Small Milk _____	
Total: _____	**Total:** _____
How much more money do you need? _____	How much more money do you need? _____
or	or
How much change will you get? _____	How much change will you get? _____

You have 80¢. Do you have enough money to buy the items listed below?	You have 94¢. Do you have enough money to buy the items listed below?
Estimate: yes _____ no _____	**Estimate:** yes _____ no _____
Actual:	**Actual:**
Chicken Noodle Soup _____	Taco _____
Carrot Sticks _____	Brownie _____
	Small Milk _____
Total: _____	**Total:** _____
How much more money do you need? _____	How much more money do you need? _____
or	or
How much change will you get? _____	How much change will you get? _____

Name _____ Date _____

Choose items from the menu to complete the bill below.
Find the amount of change you should receive. Show how
you solved the problem in the space provided.

Shooting Star Snack Shop
You have up to $1.50 to spend.

Customer's
Name:

Item   Price(¢)   _____

_____   _____

_____   _____

_____   _____

_____   _____

_____   _____   Change due

Total   _____   _____

Snack Shop Carryout 2

Use the *Shooting Star Snack Shop Children's Menu* to complete the following. You may solve the problems any way you choose, including the use of a calculator.

You have 68¢. Do you have enough money to buy the items listed below?	You have 95¢. Do you have enough money to buy the items listed below?
Estimate: yes _____ no _____	**Estimate:** yes _____ no _____
Actual:	**Actual:**
Bagel _____	Pizza Slice _____
Small Milk _____	Carrot Sticks _____
Total: _____	**Total:** _____
How much more money do you need? _____	How much more money do you need? _____
or	or
How much change will you get? _____	How much change will you get? _____

Name _____ Date _____

Choose items from the menu to complete the bill below. Find the amount of change you should receive. Show how you solved the problem in the space provided.

Shooting Star Snack Shop
You have up to $2.50 to spend.

Customer's Name:

_____

Item	Price(¢)
_____	_____
_____	_____
_____	_____
_____	_____
_____	_____

Change due _____

Total _____ _____

Snack Shop Addition and Subtraction

Unit 12

Grouping, Sharing, and Leftovers

	Student Guide	Adventure Book	Unit Resource Guide*
Lesson 1			
Grouping Numbers with Remainders	●		
Lesson 2			
In the Zoo Kitchen	●		
Lesson 3			
Monkey Treats	●		
Lesson 4			
Zoo Stickers and Stamps	●		
Lesson 5			
Zoo Lunches	●		
Lesson 6			
Writing and Solving Problems	●		

Unit Resource Guide pages are from the teacher materials.

Half-Inch Grid Paper

Half-Inch Grid Paper

Grouping Numbers with Remainders

Triangle Flash Cards: Group B Subtraction Facts

- Cut out the flash cards. To practice a subtraction fact, cover the number in the circle. Subtract the two uncovered numbers.

- Divide the cards into three piles: those facts you know and can answer quickly, those you can figure out with a strategy, and those you need to learn.

- Make a list of the facts in the last two piles. These are the facts you need to study.

- Go through all the cards again. This time cover the number in the square.

- Sort the cards into three piles again. Add the facts in the last two piles to your list that you need to study.

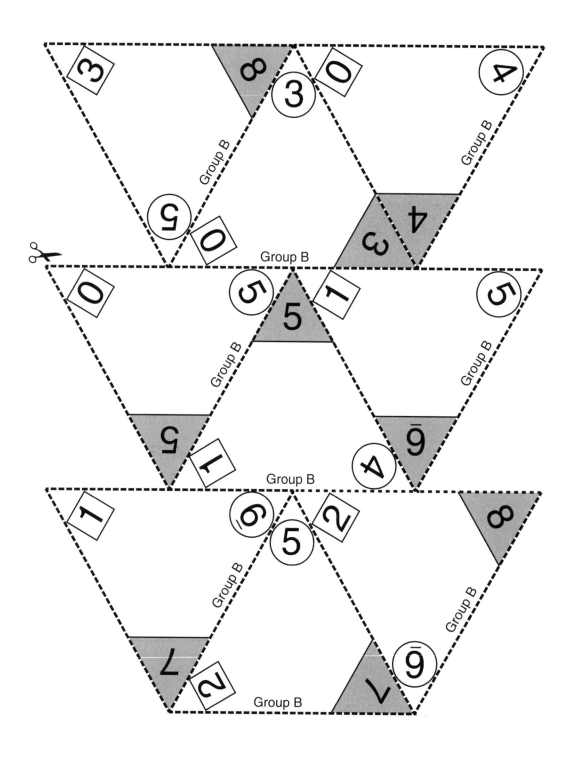

Grouping Numbers with Remainders

Children's Zoo Produce

Help the zookeeper order food for a three-day weekend. The first order slip shows how much food the zoo needs for one day.

1.

Order Slip

13 Stalks of Celery

For One Day

Order Slip

_____ **Stalks of Celery**

For Three Days

2.

Order Slip

12 Bags of Apples

For One Day

Order Slip

_____ **Bags of Apples**

For Three Days

3.

Order Slip

17 Heads of Lettuce

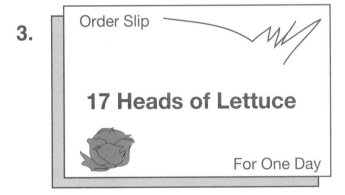

For One Day

Order Slip

_____ **Heads of Lettuce**

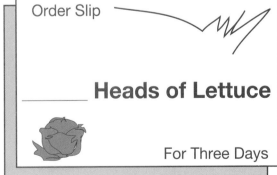

For Three Days

4.

15 Bags of Peanuts

For One Day

_____ Bags of Peanuts

For Three Days

5.

16 Bunches of Grapes

For One Day

_____ Bunches of Grapes

For Three Days

6.

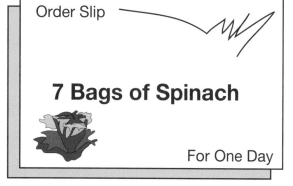

7 Bags of Spinach

For One Day

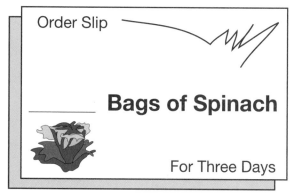

_____ Bags of Spinach

For Three Days

Great Ape House

Help the zookeeper share food for the 5 ape families. The first delivery slip shows how much food the zoo has.

1.

Delivery Slip

30 Stalks of Celery

At the Zoo

Delivery Slip

_____ **Stalks of Celery**

Per Ape Family

2.

Delivery Slip

25 Bags of Apples

At the Zoo

Delivery Slip

_____ **Bags of Apples**

Per Ape Family

3.

Delivery Slip

22 Heads of Lettuce

At the Zoo

Delivery Slip

_____ **Heads of Lettuce**

Per Ape Family

Name _____ Date _____

4.

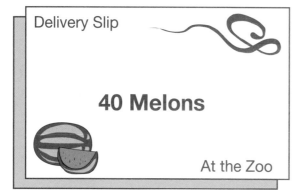
Delivery Slip

40 Melons

At the Zoo

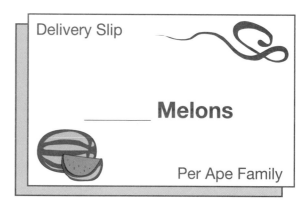
Delivery Slip

_____ **Melons**

Per Ape Family

5.

Delivery Slip

27 Boxes of Pears

At the Zoo

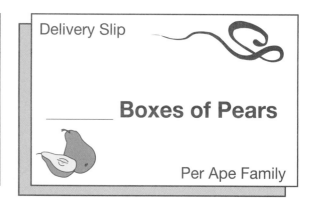
Delivery Slip

_____ **Boxes of Pears**

Per Ape Family

6.

Delivery Slip

8 Bags of Onions

At the Zoo

Delivery Slip

_____ **Bags of Onions**

Per Ape Family

In the Zoo Kitchen

Zoo Kitchen Problems

Draw pictures to solve the following problems.

1. Marcus fed 4 rabbits 2 heads of lettuce each. How many

   heads of lettuce did Marcus use? _____

2. Kristie works with horses. She feeds the horses 6 bales of
   hay each day. How many bales of hay does Kristie need for

   a three-day weekend? _____

3. Jessica has ten apples that she wants to share with the
   monkeys. There are four monkeys in the pen. How many

   apples can each monkey have? _____

Monkey Treats

Cups Spinner

$$\begin{array}{c|c} 4 & 2 \\ \hline 3 & 1 \end{array}$$

Players

This is a game for two or more players.

Materials

Monkey Treats Recording Sheet

Rules

1. Spin the Cups Spinner to find how many cups to set out for the monkeys. (Use a pencil and paper clip.)

2. Spin the Peanuts Spinner to find how many peanuts to put in each cup. Use cubes to stand for peanuts.

Peanuts Spinner

$$\begin{array}{c|c} 10 & 2 \\ \hline 3 & 5 \end{array}$$

3. Turn to the *Monkey Treats Recording Sheet* on the next page. Draw a picture that shows the number of cups and peanuts you spin.

4. Write a multiplication sentence that describes your cups and peanuts.

5. Add the peanuts column. How many peanuts did the zookeeper give the monkeys?

Multiplication Sentences

Spin	Cups		Peanuts in Each Cup		Peanuts
Monday		$\times$		=	
Tuesday		$\times$		=	
Wednesday		$\times$		=	
Thursday		$\times$		=	
Friday		$\times$		=	

6. The player with the most monkey treats after writing five number sentences wins!

Name _____   Date _____

Monkey Treats Recording Sheet

Draw pictures showing the number of cups and peanuts you spin. An example is provided for you.

Example: My spinners show 3 cups with 5 peanuts each.

Monday:

Tuesday:

Wednesday:

Thursday:

Friday:

Name _____ Date _____

How Many?

Draw a picture for each problem. Then write a number sentence to answer the question.

1. Draw 6 monkey faces.

How many eyes are there in all? _____

2. Draw 3 cars.

How many tires are there in all? _____

3. Draw 4 tricycles.

How many wheels are there in all? _____

---

4. Draw your own picture about equal groups.

How many _____ are there in all? _____

Zoo Problems

Use drawings to solve Questions 1–4. Write a number sentence to show how you solved the problem.

1. Jerry had 4 apples and 3 bananas. How many pieces of fruit

   did he have? _____

2. There were 4 monkeys. Each monkey had 3 bananas. How

   many bananas were there altogether? _____

3. There are 4 sea lions, 3 polar bears, and 3 seals in the pool. What is the total number of animals in the pool?

_____

4. There were 6 apes. Each ape had 3 apples. How many

apples were there altogether? _____

Zoo Stickers

**Mario, Jacob, and Lisa each bought a sheet of zoo stickers.
How many stickers did each student buy? Write a number
sentence to show your answer.**

Mario

Jacob

Lisa

Name _____   Date _____

Zoo Stamps

Mary Beth, Tony, and Shana each bought a page of zoo
stamps. Write a number sentence to show how you found the
answers to the questions below.

Mary Beth

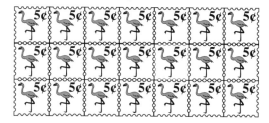

1. How many stamps did Mary Beth buy?

   _____

2. How much did all of her stamps cost?

   _____

Tony

Shana

3. How many stamps did Tony buy?

   _____

4. Total cost? _____

5. How many stamps did Shana buy?

   _____

6. Total cost? _____

Collection of Stickers and Stamps

Homework

1. Terry bought a page of giraffe stickers.

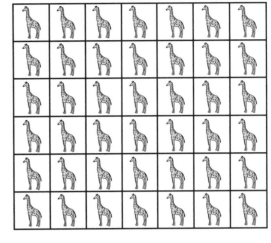

   A. How many stickers did he buy? Use a number sentence to show your answer.

   _____

   B. Terry wants to give half of his stickers to his little sister. How many stickers will Terry have left? Show how you found your answer.

   _____

   _____

2. Draw a page of stickers with three rows. Draw four stickers in each row. Write a number sentence to show the total number of stickers on the page.

3. **A.** Kelly has $1.00.
Which page
of stamps can
she buy? Show
how you found
your answer.

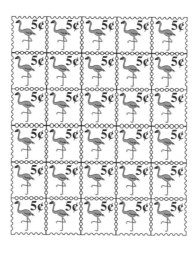

B. How much money would Kelly have left? Explain
your thinking.

_____

_____

_____

C. Kelly wants to buy both pages of stamps. How much
more money does she need? Show how you solved
this problem.

_____

_____

_____

Lunchtime at the Bird House

It is lunchtime at the Bird House. Help the zookeeper share the food. Draw pictures to show how many items each bird will get.

1. Draw 6 bird bowls. Share 18 orange segments.

How many will each bird get? _____

---

2. Draw 3 bird bowls. Share 12 grapes.

How many will each bird get? _____

3. Draw 4 bird bowls. Share 10 leaves of spinach.

How many will each bird get? _____

---

4. Draw 5 bird bowls. Share 20 bananas.

How many will each bird get? _____

---

5. Draw 2 bird bowls. Share 14 seeds.

How many will each bird get? _____

Fruits and Vegetables for the Reptile House

Shipments	Daily Amount Needed	Number of Days Food Will Last
10 bags of zucchini	2 bags	
25 bags of apples	5 bags	
17 bunches of carrots	4 bunches	
12 bags of kale	3 bags	
16 bags of beans	2 bags	
11 bags of lettuce	2 bags	

Name _____ Date _____

It's for the Birds

Help the mother bird share the food with her babies.

1. Each baby bird needs 2 leaves of spinach. Mother bird has 10 leaves. Draw the number of baby birds she can feed.

How many baby birds ate spinach? _____

2. Each baby bird needs 4 grapes. Mother bird has 12 grapes. Draw the number of baby birds she can feed.

How many baby birds ate grapes? _____

3. Each baby bird needs 4 apple chunks. Mother bird has
12 apple chunks. Draw the number of baby birds she can feed.

How many baby birds ate apple chunks? _____

---

4. Each baby bird needs 5 raisins. Mother bird has 16 raisins.
Draw the number of baby birds she can feed.

How many baby birds ate raisins? _____

---

5. Each baby bird needs 8 seeds. Mother bird has 24 seeds.
Draw the number of baby birds she can feed.

How many baby birds ate seeds? _____

A Problem I Saw

Homework

What did you see on your way home from school today? Write a multiplication or a division problem about some of these things. Bring it to school for the rest of your class to solve. Draw a picture to show what you are multiplying or dividing.

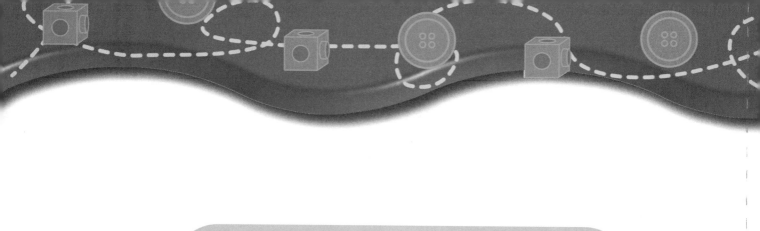

Unit 13

Sampling, Sorting, and Science

	Student Guide	Adventure Book	Unit Resource Guide*
Lesson 1			
Classifying and Sorting Lids	●		
Lesson 2			
Monkey Business		●	
Lesson 3			
Two-Variable Sorting	●		
Lesson 4			
Undercover Investigation	●		

Unit Resource Guide pages are from the teacher materials.

Classifying and Sorting Lids

Use your sample of lids. What will you study about your lids? I will study…

_____

_____

Draw a picture. Show how you will sort the lids. Show the variable and the groups for sorting. Write the names of the groups.

Lids Data Table

Sort your lids. Record the data below.

Lids

	N Number

Make a bar graph of your data on graph paper.

What does the graph show you about the lids in your sample?
Write about it.

_____

_____

_____

Name _____   Date _____

Recycling Lids

Tina and James collected lids from their homes. Then they sorted them by material. They put their data in a table.

Lid Material

M Material	N Number
metal only	35
metal with rubber inside	10
plastic	51
paper	3

Show how you solved each problem.

1. What was the least common type of lid material?

_____

2. How many more plastic lids than paper lids were there?

_____

3. How many more plastic lids than lids with metal were there?

_____

_____

4. How many lids did Tina and James collect?

_____

_____

5. Were more than half of the lids made of plastic? Explain.

_____

_____

_____

Triangle Flash Cards: Group C Subtraction Facts

- Cut out the flash cards. To practice a subtraction fact, cover the number in the circle. Subtract the two uncovered numbers.

- Divide the cards into three piles: those facts you know and can answer quickly, those you can figure out with a strategy, and those you need to learn.

- Make a list of the facts in the last two piles. These are the facts you need to study.

- Go through all the cards again. This time cover the number in the square.

- Sort the cards into three piles again. Add the facts in the last two piles to your list that you need to study.

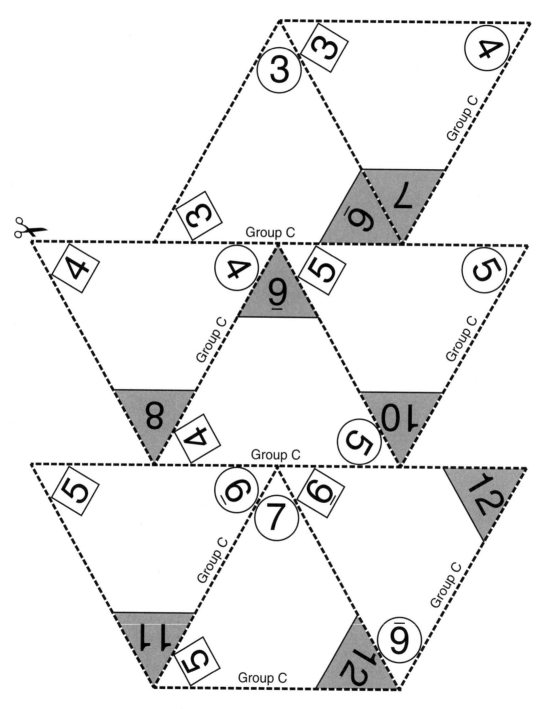

Name _____   Date _____

Two-Variable Sorting

Using your sample of lids, what do you want to find out?

Purpose: I want to find out _____

_____

**Draw a picture. Show how you will sort the lids two ways.
Show the two variables and the groups for sorting each variable.
Write the names of the variables and the names of the groups.**

Work with your partner. Decide how to organize your data for sorting two variables. Draw your data tables and fill them in.

Name _____ Date _____

Keenya and Michael's Lids

Keenya and Michael chose to find out if metal lids were the same size as plastic lids.

They sorted their lids. Then they made the two data tables on the next page.

Use the tables on the following page to answer the questions.

1. Are there more small, medium, or large lids? _____

2. What is the most common size of plastic lids? _____

Metal Lids

S Size	N Number
small	7
medium	5
large	29

Plastic Lids

S Size	N Number
small	3
medium	30
large	8

3. What is the most common size of metal lids? _____

4. Are there more metal lids or plastic lids? _____

5. How could you organize Keenya and Michael's data another way? Draw your tables below.

Frank and Kaley's Lids

Frank and Kaley chose to study the material and color of their lids. They made two data tables.

Lid Material

M Material	N Number
plastic	57
metal	33

Lid Color

C Color	N Number
white	11
red	5
blue	23
silver	17
gold	24
other	10

Use the tables to answer the questions.

1. What is the most common color? _____

2. How many lids are there altogether? How did you find your

   answer? _____

   _____

3. What is another way to find out how many lids there are?

   _____

   _____

4. Can you tell how many of the plastic lids are red?

   Explain. _____

   _____

Discuss

Frank and Kaley want to compare the color of metal lids and plastic lids. Discuss with your partner or group other ways to make data tables for the study. Show your new data tables below.

Name _____ Date _____

Undercover Investigation

Purpose: My class wants to find out _____
_____

Draw a picture. Show the two variables and the groups for sorting each variable. Write the names of the variables and the names of the groups.

Name _____   Date _____

What data tables will you need? Draw the data tables your class decides to use. Sort your lids. Record the data.

What bar graphs will you make? Decide with your class. Make your graphs on separate sheets of graph paper.

1. Study your class data. What does it tell you about the lids?

    _____

    _____

    _____

    _____

2. Compare your class results to the data you and your partner collected. Are the data similar?

    _____

    _____

    _____

Name _____ Date _____

Megan and Danny's Lids

Megan and Danny sorted a sample of lids. They recorded their data.

Use the data to answer the questions.

Metal Lids

S Size	N Number	
small	||||| ||||| ||	12
medium	|||	3
large	|||||		6

Plastic Lids

S Size	N Number	
small	||||| ||||	9
medium	|||||	5
large	||||| ||	7

1. How many small plastic lids are there? _____

2. How many metal lids are there? _____

3. How many lids are there altogether? _____

4. How many medium-size lids are there? _____

5. Which table has twice as many small lids as large lids?

   _____

6. Predict the number of large plastic lids there might be if the sample were doubled.

   _____

Mena Sorts for Recycling

Mena collects lids to be recycled. She sorts them by color and material. Here is the data table she made for this week. Use her data to answer the questions.

M **Material**	**C** **Color**		
	Gold	**Black**	**White**
metal	7	2	3
plastic	14	7	20

1. **A.** Are there more black lids or white lids?

   _____

   B. How many more?

   _____

2. **A.** Are there more gold lids or white lids?

   _____

   B. How many more?

   _____

3. Which color has the greatest number of lids?

_____

4. Which color has the fewest number of lids?

_____

5. A. Are there more plastic lids or metal lids?

_____

  B. How many more?

_____

  C. Is it more than twice as many more?

_____

6. Mena collected twice as many lids last week. Estimate the number of plastic lids that she collected last week. Explain how you got that number.

_____

_____

_____

Undercover Investigation

Unit 14

Fractions: The Whole Idea

	Student Guide	Adventure Book	Unit Resource Guide*
Lesson 1			
Folding Fractions	●		
Lesson 2			
Fraction Puzzles	●		
Lesson 3			
Tile Fraction Puzzles	●		
Lesson 4			
Fraction Games	●		

Unit Resource Guide pages are from the teacher materials.

Name _____ Date _____

Granola Bar Fractions

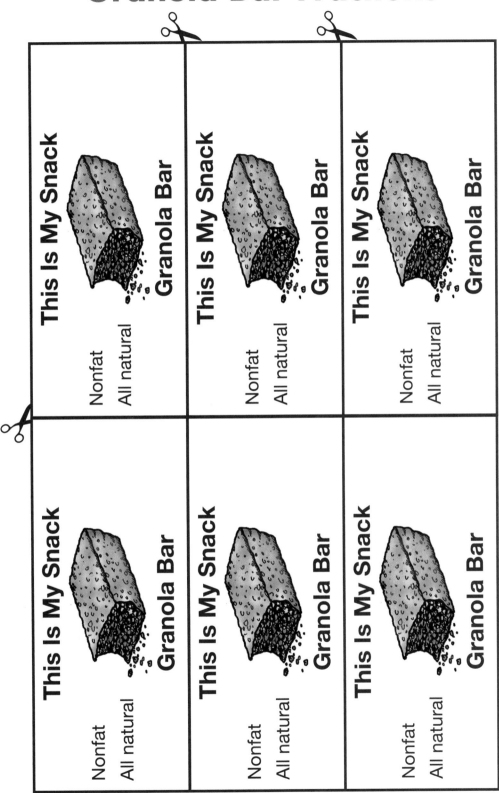

Folding Fractions

Fraction Strips

Cut out the fraction strips along the bold lines.

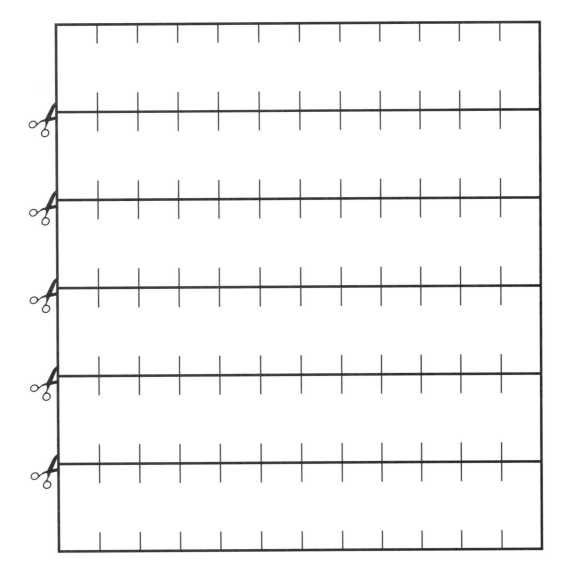

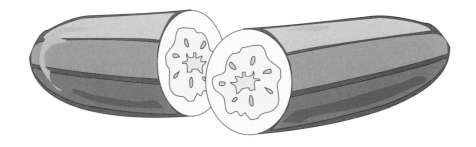

Name _____ Date _____

Folding Fractions

Folding Fractions on Our Own

Use fraction strips to make these fractions. Write the symbol for each fraction on the strip.

1. one-third

2. one-fourth

3. two-fourths

4. three-thirds

5. two-halves

6. zero-thirds

7. three-fourths

8. one-half

9. four-fourths

Name _____ Date _____

Banana Split

After buying a banana at a local fruit store,
Jess and Bess started squabbling about who would get more.

"Let's cut it in half," said the first to the other.
"We'll each have two pieces and none for our brother."

"Hold on one minute!" the second one cried.
"I think we'll get more if we further divide.

Halves means two pieces. In fourths, there are four.
If we split the fruit that way, we're bound to get more!"

"But if fourths are good, then eighths must be great!"
So, they both got four pieces, which each of them ate.

**Do Jess and Bess understand fractions?
Explain. You may wish to draw a picture
to help explain your thinking.**

_____

_____

_____

_____

Triangle Flash Cards: Group D Subtraction Facts

- Cut out the flash cards. To practice a subtraction fact, cover the number in the circle. Subtract the two uncovered numbers.

- Divide the cards into three piles: those facts you know and can answer quickly, those you can figure out with a strategy, and those you need to learn.

- Make a list of the facts in the last two piles. These are the facts you need to study.

- Go through all the cards again. This time cover the number in the square.

- Sort the cards into three piles again. Add the facts in the last two piles to your list that you need to study.

Folding Fractions

One-Half Plus One-Fourth 1

1. What fraction is shown in green on square A? _____

2. What fraction is shown in green on square C? _____

3. What fraction is shown in green on square D? _____

Cut out the shaded parts in squares C and D. Then paste them on square B to look like square A.

Write a number sentence to describe square B.

A

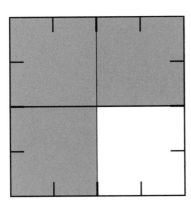

B

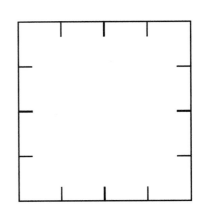

C

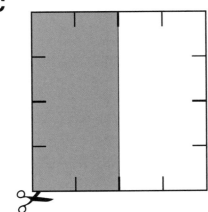

D

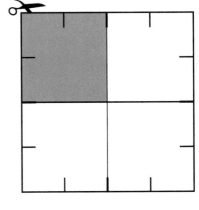

One-Half Plus One-Fourth 2

1. What fraction is shown in red on square A? _____

2. What fraction is shown in red on square C? _____

3. What fraction is shown in red on square D? _____

Cut out the shaded parts in squares C and D. Then paste them on square B to look like square A.

Write a number sentence that describes your answer.

A

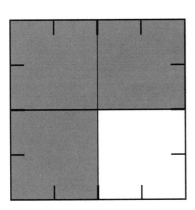

B

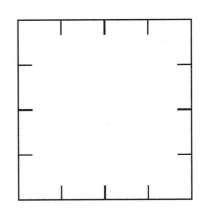

C

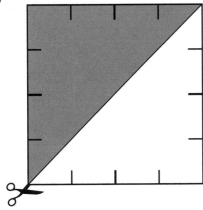

D

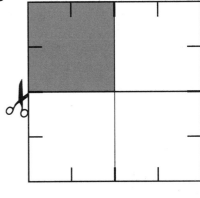

Name _____ Date _____

One-Half Plus One-Fourth 3

1. What fraction is shown in yellow on square A? _____

2. What fraction is shown in yellow on square C? _____

3. What fraction is shown in yellow on square D? _____

Cut out the shaded parts in squares C and D. Then paste them on square B to look like square A.

Write a number sentence that describes your answer.

A

B

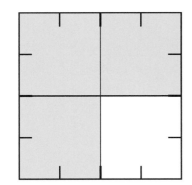

C

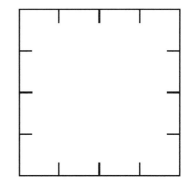

D

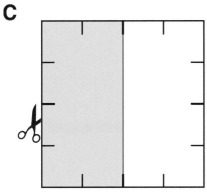

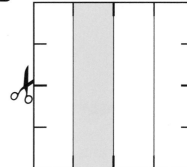

Puzzle Proof

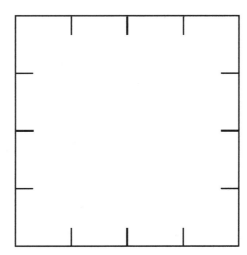

Both A and B show the fraction three-fourths ($\frac{3}{4}$). Cut up one of the squares below. Paste it on the square above to show that the shaded parts cover the same amount of space.

$$\frac{3}{4}$$

$$\frac{3}{4}$$

A

B

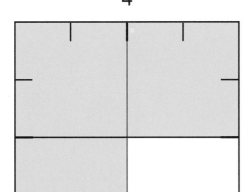

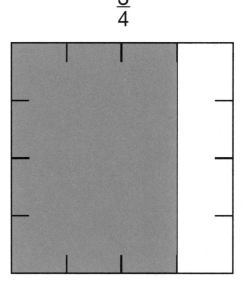

Tile Fraction Puzzles 1

Follow the directions for covering each shape with tiles. Then color each shape to show how you covered it.

1. one-half red and one-half green

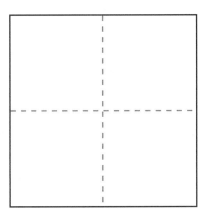

2. one-third blue and two-thirds yellow

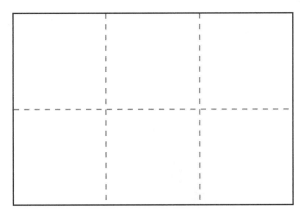

3. one-fourth red and three-fourths blue

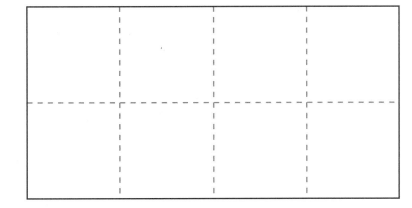

Tile Fraction Puzzles 2

Continue working as you did in *Tile Fraction Puzzles 1.*

1. one-fourth red, one-fourth yellow, and one-half green

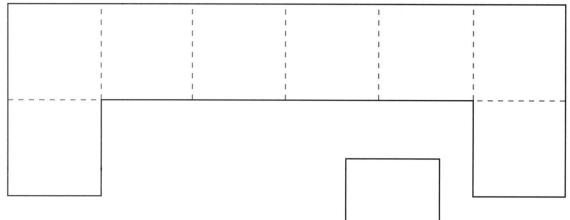

2. one-half yellow and one-half blue

3. one-third blue and two-thirds yellow

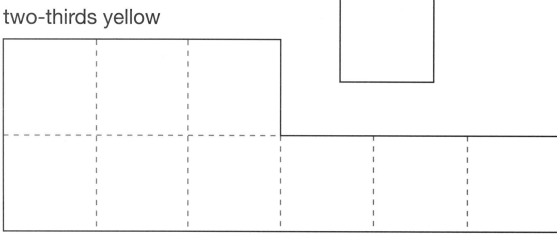

Tile Fraction Puzzles 3

Continue working as you did in *Tile Fraction Puzzles 1* and 2.

1. one-half green and
   one-half yellow

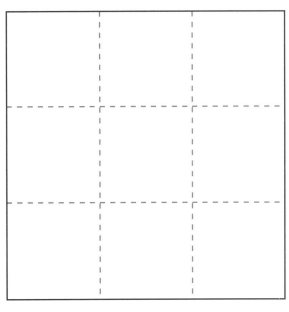

2. Use your tiles to make your own shape one-half blue and one-half green. Then draw and color your shape on the dots below.

More Tile Fraction Puzzles

1. Color one-third green and two-thirds yellow.

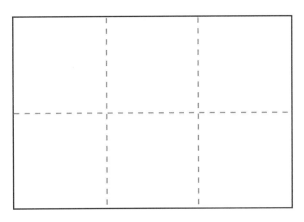

2. Draw and color a shape that is covered with square-inch tiles one-half blue and one-half yellow.

Halves Cards

two-halves	one-half	one-half	two-halves
two-halves	one-half	one-half	two-halves
two-halves	zero-halves	zero-halves	zero-halves
two-halves	zero-halves	zero-halves	zero-halves
$\frac{1}{2}$	$\frac{1}{2}$	$\frac{1}{2}$	$\frac{2}{2}$
$\frac{1}{2}$	$\frac{1}{2}$	$\frac{1}{2}$	$\frac{2}{2}$

Name _____ Date _____

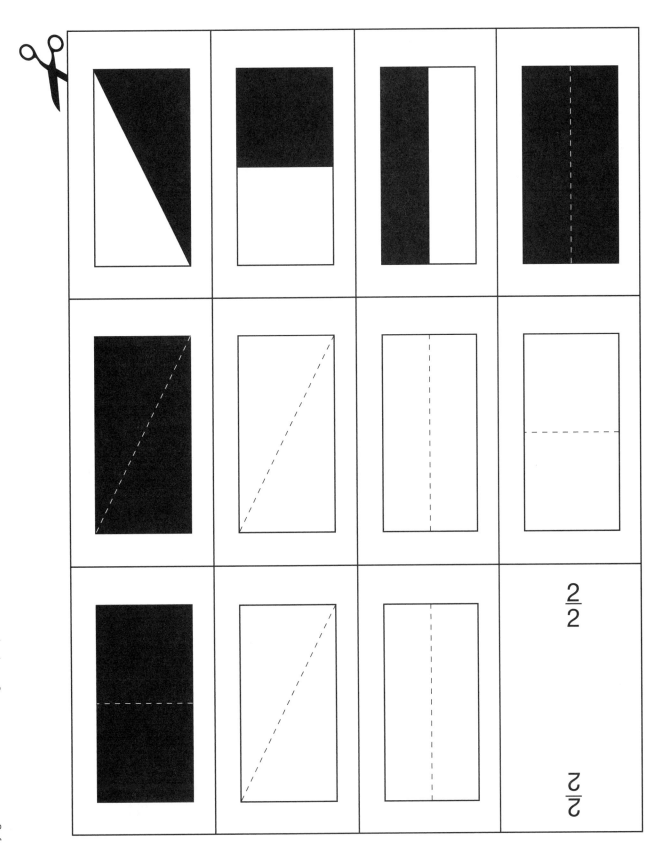

$$\frac{2}{2}$$

$$\frac{2}{2}$$

Fraction Games

Name ____________________ Date ____________

Fourths Cards

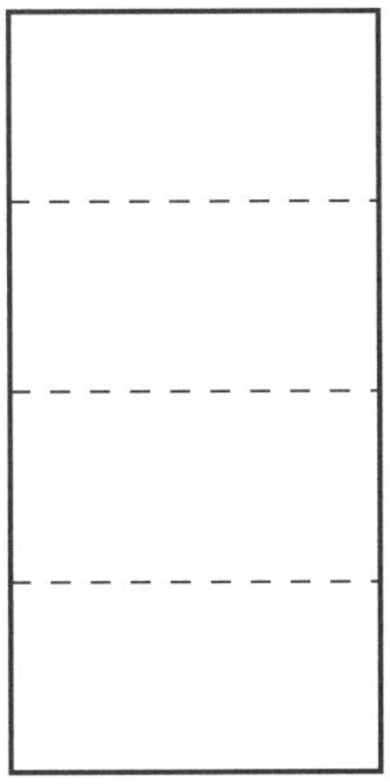
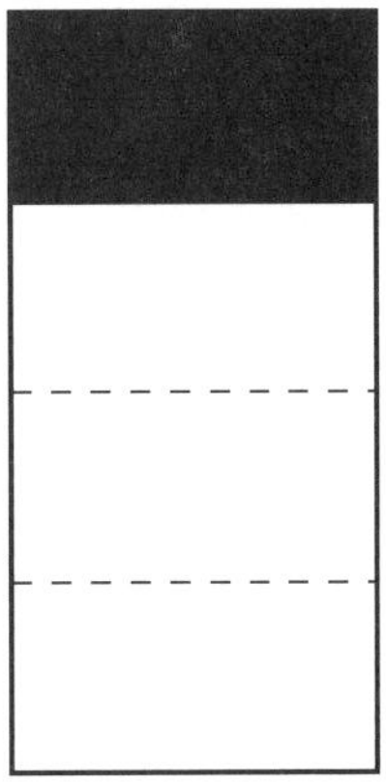

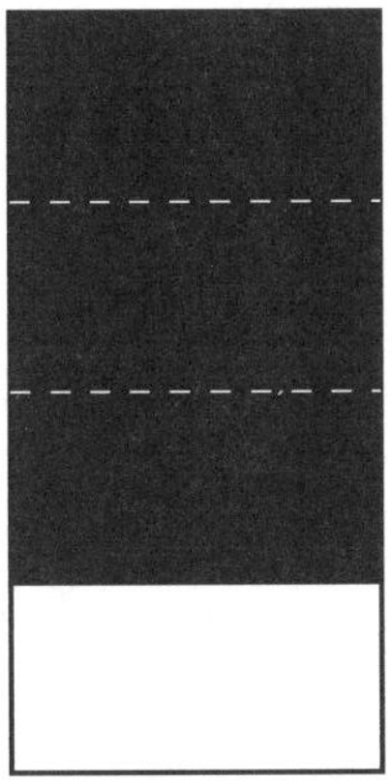

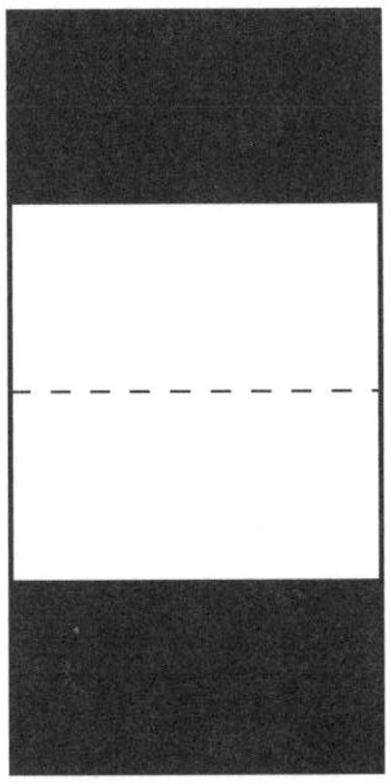

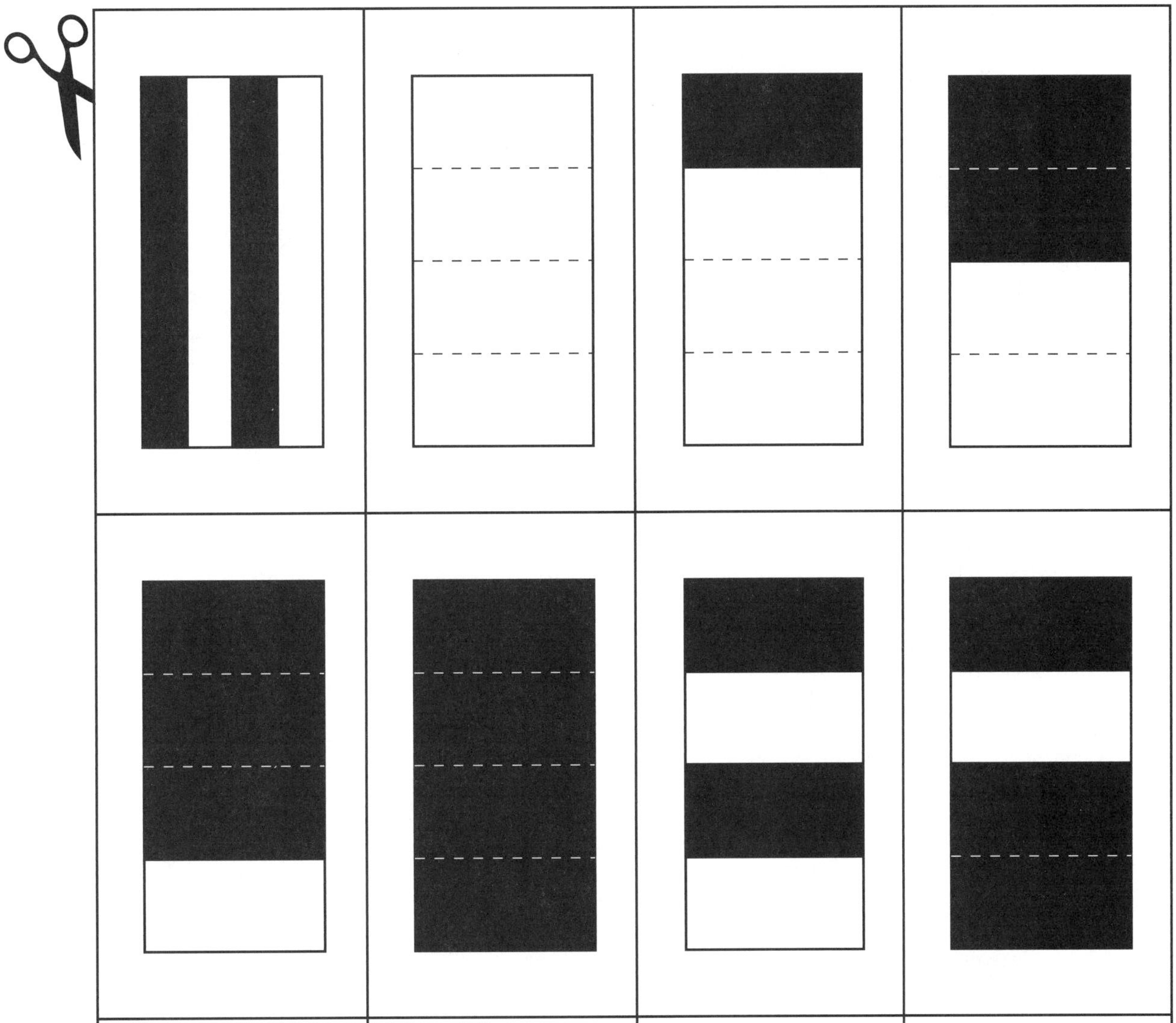

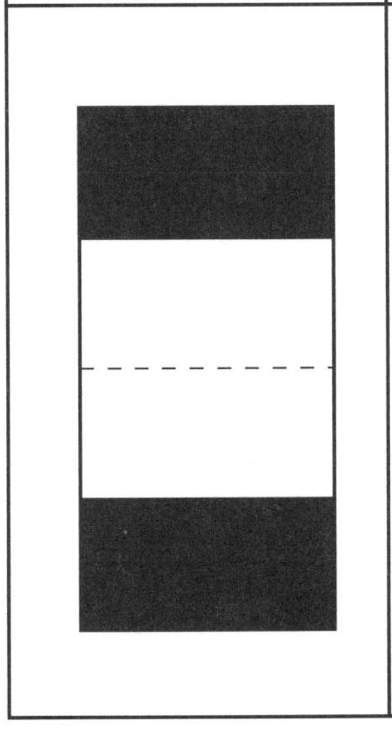

$\frac{2}{4}$

$\frac{2}{4}$

$\frac{0}{4}$

$\frac{0}{4}$

$\frac{0}{4}$

$\frac{0}{4}$

Name ______________________ Date ____________

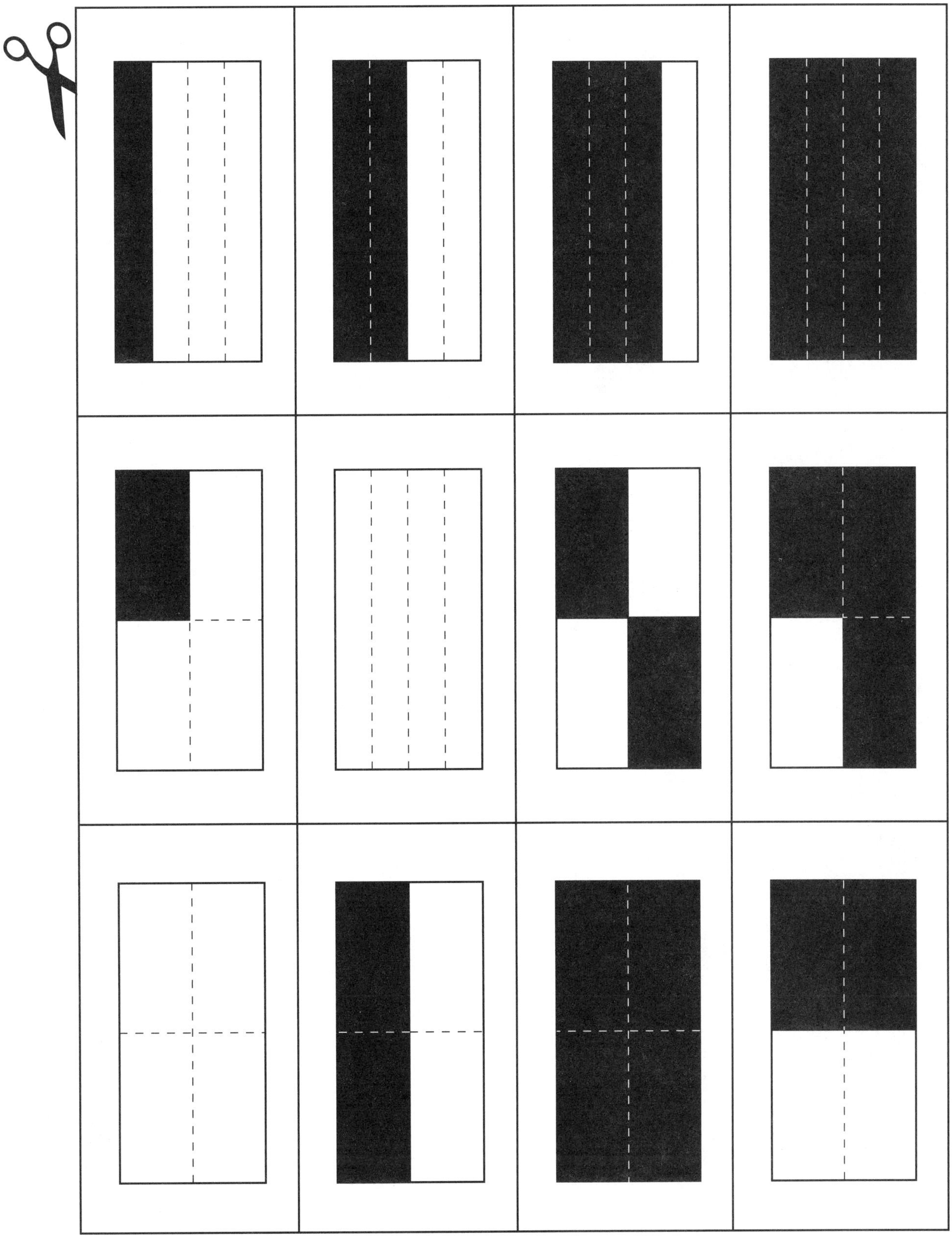

Name _____   Date _____

two-fourths	zero-fourths	one-fourth	two-fourths
two-fourths	zero-fourths	one-fourth	two-fourths
three-fourths	four-fourths		
three-fourths	four-fourths		
one-fourth	zero-fourths		
one-fourth	zero-fourths		

two-fourths	four-fourths	two-fourths	three-fourths
two-fourths	four-fourths	two-fourths	three-fourths
$\frac{2}{4}$	$\frac{0}{4}$	$\frac{1}{4}$	$\frac{2}{4}$
$\frac{2}{4}$	$\frac{0}{4}$	$\frac{1}{4}$	$\frac{2}{4}$
$\frac{3}{4}$	$\frac{4}{4}$	$\frac{2}{4}$	$\frac{3}{4}$
$\frac{3}{4}$	$\frac{4}{4}$	$\frac{2}{4}$	$\frac{3}{4}$

$\dfrac{1}{4}$	$\dfrac{2}{4}$	$\dfrac{3}{4}$	$\dfrac{4}{4}$
$\dfrac{1}{4}$	$\dfrac{2}{4}$	$\dfrac{3}{4}$	$\dfrac{4}{4}$
$\dfrac{1}{4}$	$\dfrac{0}{4}$	$\dfrac{2}{4}$	$\dfrac{3}{4}$
$\dfrac{1}{4}$	$\dfrac{0}{4}$	$\dfrac{2}{4}$	$\dfrac{3}{4}$
$\dfrac{0}{4}$	$\dfrac{2}{4}$	$\dfrac{4}{4}$	$\dfrac{2}{4}$
$\dfrac{0}{4}$	$\dfrac{2}{4}$	$\dfrac{4}{4}$	$\dfrac{2}{4}$

Thirds Cards

$\frac{3}{3}$	$\frac{2}{3}$	$\frac{1}{3}$	$\frac{0}{3}$
$\frac{3}{3}$	$\frac{2}{3}$	$\frac{1}{3}$	$\frac{0}{3}$
$\frac{2}{3}$	$\frac{2}{3}$	$\frac{3}{3}$	$\frac{2}{3}$
$\frac{2}{3}$	$\frac{2}{3}$	$\frac{3}{3}$	$\frac{2}{3}$
$\frac{1}{3}$	$\frac{0}{3}$	$\frac{1}{3}$	$\frac{1}{3}$
$\frac{1}{3}$	$\frac{0}{3}$	$\frac{1}{3}$	$\frac{1}{3}$

		zero-thirds	one-third
		spɹᴉɥʇ-oɹǝz	pɹᴉɥʇ-ǝuo
		three-thirds	two-thirds
		spɹᴉɥʇ-ǝǝɹɥʇ	spɹᴉɥʇ-oʍʇ
zero-thirds	one-third	two-thirds	three-thirds
spɹᴉɥʇ-oɹǝz	pɹᴉɥʇ-ǝuo	spɹᴉɥʇ-oʍʇ	spɹᴉɥʇ-ǝǝɹɥʇ

Name _____ Date _____

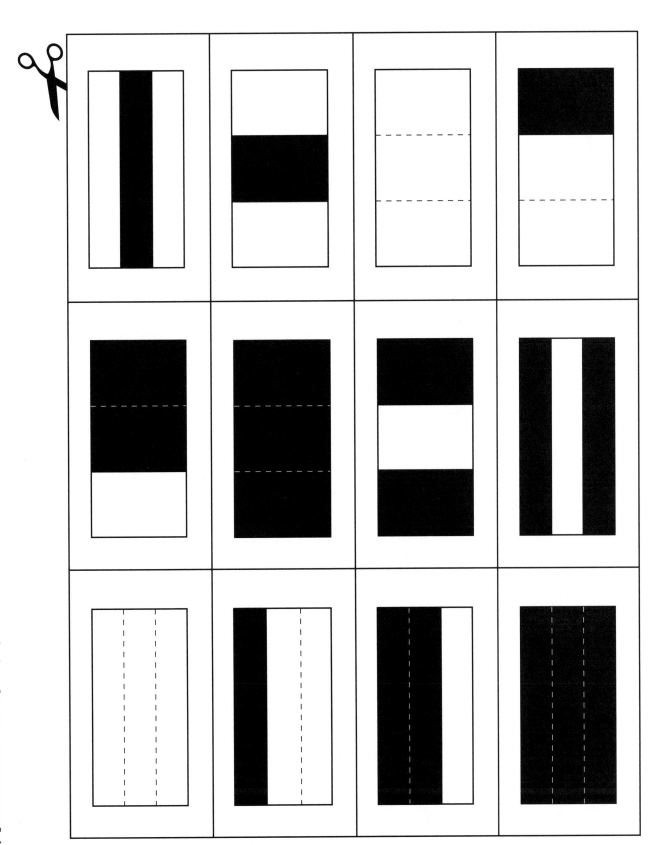

Fraction Games

Homework

Dear Family Member:

We learned two fraction games in class: *Fraction War* and *Fraction Concentration*. Ask your child to teach these games to family members at home. Please help your child keep a record of the number of people he or she teaches to play the games and for how long they play the games.

Thank you.

Fraction War

Tally for Each Person	Tally for Each 5 Minutes

Fraction Concentration

Tally for Each Person	Tally for Each 5 Minutes

Family member's signature _____

Child's signature _____

Return this sheet to school by _____

Fraction War

Players

This is a game for two players.

Materials

- *Halves Cards*   • *Fourths Cards*   • *Thirds Cards*

Rules

1. One player deals out all the cards, half to each player.
2. Each player lays his or her stack face down in a pile.
3. Each player turns over one card.
4. The player with the larger fraction takes both cards.
5. If the fractions are the same size, it is a war.
6. For a war, each player puts a second card face down and a third face up.
7. The player whose third card represents the larger fraction takes all the cards.
8. Cards that are won are added to the bottom of the player's pile.
9. Play for 10 minutes or until one player runs out of cards.
10. The player with the most cards at the end of the game wins.

Fraction Concentration

Players

This is a game for two or more players.

Materials

- *Halves Cards*   • *Fourths Cards*   • *Thirds Cards*

Rules

1. Players lay out all the cards face down in a big rectangle.
2. The first player turns over any two cards.
3. If the cards match, the player picks them up and takes another turn. A match is two cards that both represent the same fraction. For example, a card with a rectangle that represents one-fourth and a card with the fraction $\frac{1}{4}$ are a match.
4. If the cards do not match, the player turns them face down, and the next player takes a turn.
5. The player with the most cards at the end of the game wins.

How Are All These Alike?

Tell how each fraction is like the other.

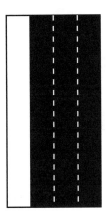

three-fourths
$\frac{3}{4}$

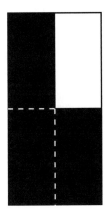

_____

_____

_____

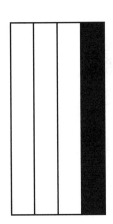

one-fourth
$\frac{1}{4}$

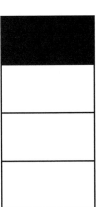

_____

_____

_____

Unit 15

Geometry in Motion

	Student Guide	Adventure Book	Unit Resource Guide*
Lesson 1			
Getting to Know Shapes	●		
Lesson 2			
Getting to Know More about Shapes	●		●
Lesson 3			
Professor Peabody Visits Flatville	●		
Lesson 4			
Symmetry	●		
Lesson 5			
Quilt Blocks	●		

Unit Resource Guide pages are from the teacher materials.

417

Triangle Flash Cards: Group E Subtraction Facts

- Cut out the flash cards. To practice a subtraction fact, cover the number in the circle. Subtract the two uncovered numbers.

- Divide the cards into three piles: those facts you know and can answer quickly, those you can figure out with a strategy, and those you need to learn.

- Make a list of the facts in the last two piles. These are the facts you need to study.

- Go through all the cards again. This time cover the number in the square.

- Sort the cards into three piles again. Add the facts in the last two piles to your list that you need to study.

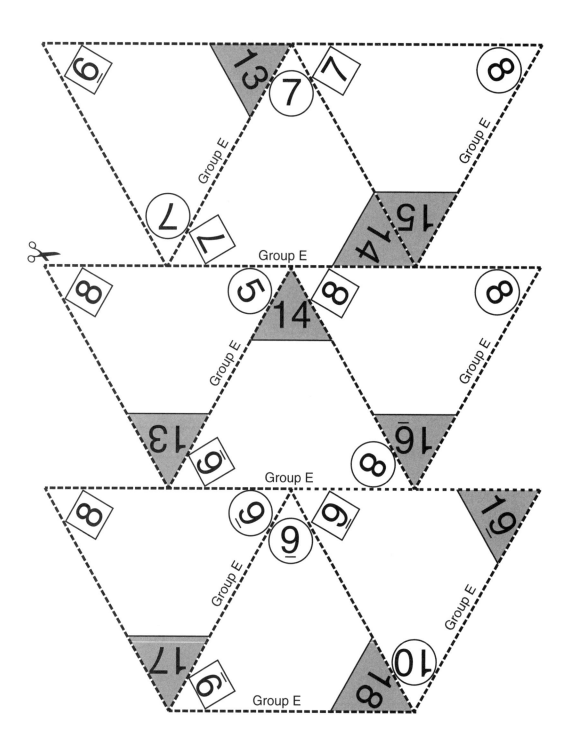

Getting to Know Shapes

Name _____

Date _____

Shapes Grid

Use yes or no to answer each question on the grid.

Pattern Block Shape	Are opposite sides parallel?	Are opposite sides equal length?	Are all the sides of equal length?	How many sides are there?	Do all the corners look the same?
hexagon					
trapezoid					
triangle	✕	✕			
square					
blue rhombus					
tan rhombus					

What Shape Am I?

Homework

Use the *Shapes Grid* you completed to solve the riddles.

1. I have four sides. They are all the same length. What shape(s) can I be?

   _____

2. My four sides are the same length. I also have square corners. What shape(s) can I be?

   _____

3. Two of my sides are parallel to one another. The other two sides are not. What shape(s) can I be?

   _____

4. All of my sides are the same length. All my corners look the same too. What shape(s) can I be?

   _____

5. Two of the triangle pattern blocks can be put together to form me. What shape(s) can I be?

   _____

6. Write your own riddle. Give it to a friend to solve.

   _____

   _____

Professor Peabody Visits Flatville

Professor Peabody is visiting Flatville. Everything in Flatville is two-dimensional or flat—even the people! They are called Flatniks. The first person Professor Peabody met was a scientist named Professor Ima Rectangle.

I am visiting Flatville so I can tell my friends on Earth what it's like. Can you show me around?

Sure! But don't tell anyone you're from Earth. Flatniks think Earth is just a fairy tale. They think it's impossible to have three dimensions.

People in Flatville have three ways of moving around. One way is called **sliding.** Watch what happens if Professor Rectangle slides east.

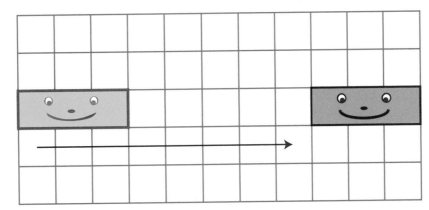

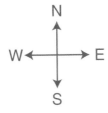

N
W ← → E
S

Another way of moving is called **turning.** Tell how Professor Rectangle moved to get into the library.

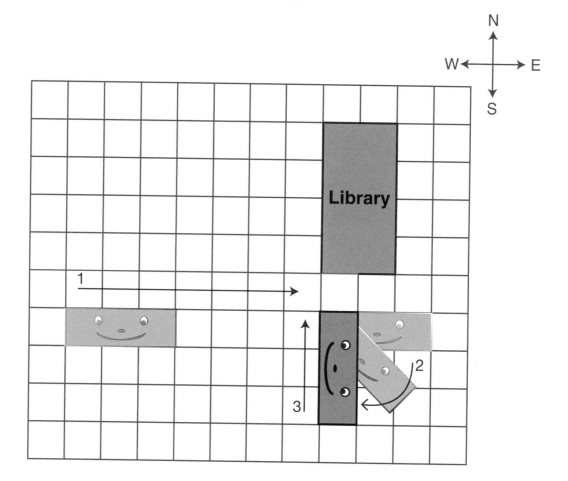

_____

_____

_____

_____

Professor Peabody Visits Flatville

Professor Rectangle bought a car. She tried to park it in her garage by moving with slides and turns. It would not fit.

Cut out Professor Rectangle's Car. Use slides and turns to try to park it in her garage.

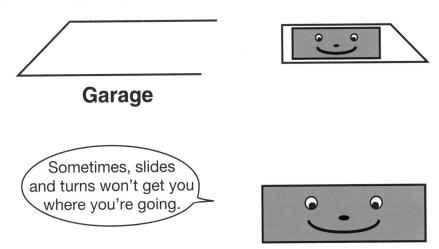

Garage

Sometimes, slides and turns won't get you where you're going.

Professor Rectangle has to use the Flip-O-Tron machine to get into her garage. Pressing the Flip-O-Tron button causes an object in Flatville to get **flipped.** Notice what happened to Professor Rectangle's car after it was flipped. Now it fits in her garage.

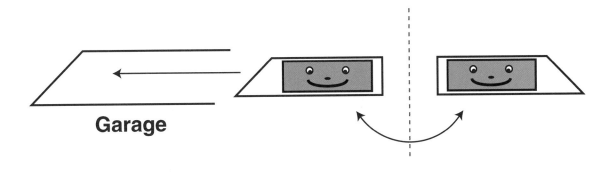

Garage

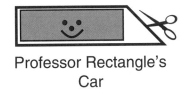

Professor Rectangle's Car

Professor Rectangle's Neighborhood

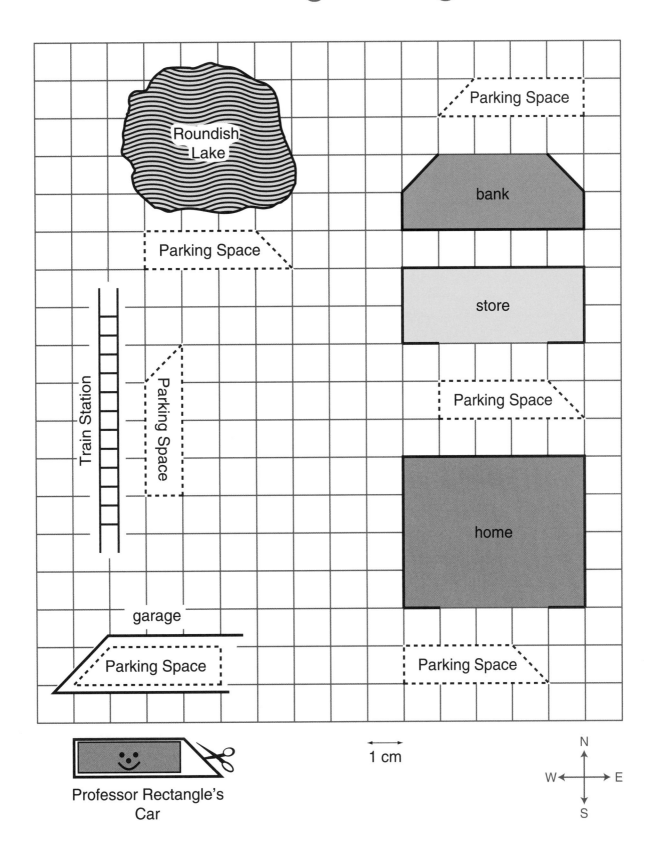

Roundish Lake

Parking Space

bank

Parking Space

store

Train Station

Parking Space

Parking Space

home

garage

Parking Space

Parking Space

1 cm

N
W ← → E
S

Professor Rectangle's Car

Kiddie Rectangle Around Town

Use slides, turns, and flips to move Kiddie's car.

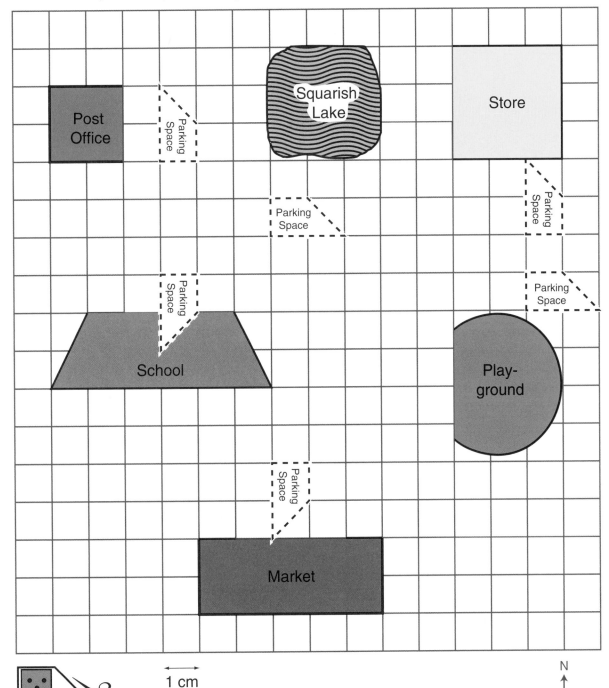

1 cm

Kiddie's car

N
W ← → E
S

For each question, the car moves from a parking space to a parking space.

Example: How does Kiddie's car get from the Market to Squarish Lake?

Slide 7 cm north. Turn east. _____

_____

1. How does Kiddie's car get from Squarish Lake to the School?

_____

_____

2. How does Kiddie's car get from the School to the Post Office?

_____

_____

3. How does Kiddie's car get from the Post Office to the Store?

_____

_____

4. How does Kiddie's car get from the Store to the Market?

_____

_____

5. Make up and solve your own problem.

_____

_____

Kiddie Rectangle Visits Grandma

Use slides, flips, and turns to move Kiddie's car. Kiddie's car can slide forward or sideways.

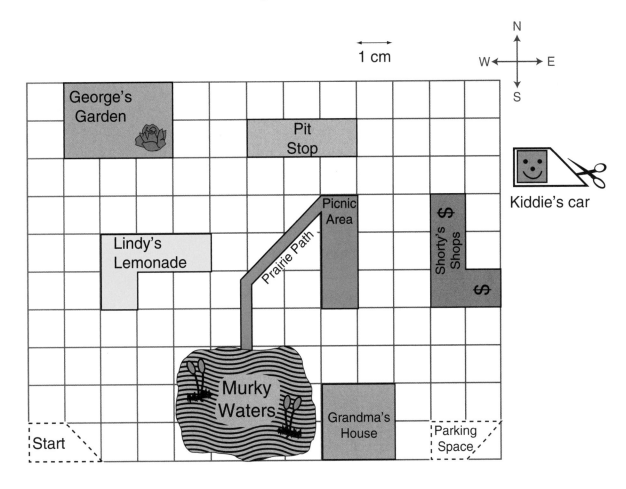

Cut out Kiddie's car. Place it on Start. Write a story. Tell how Kiddie's car can travel to the parking space for Grandma's house using slides, flips, and turns.

_____

_____

_____

Line and Turn Symmetry 1

Cut out the shapes.

1. Fold the shapes to see if they have a line of symmetry.

2. Unfold the shapes. Cover them with pattern blocks.

3. Which shape or shapes have turn symmetry?

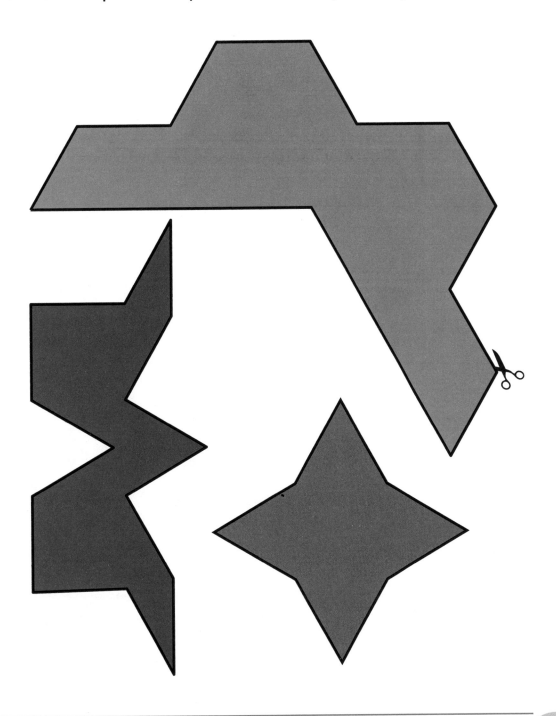

Line and Turn Symmetry 2

Cut out the shapes.

1. Fold the shapes to see if they have a line of symmetry.

2. Unfold the shapes. Cover them with pattern blocks.

3. Which shape or shapes have turn symmetry?

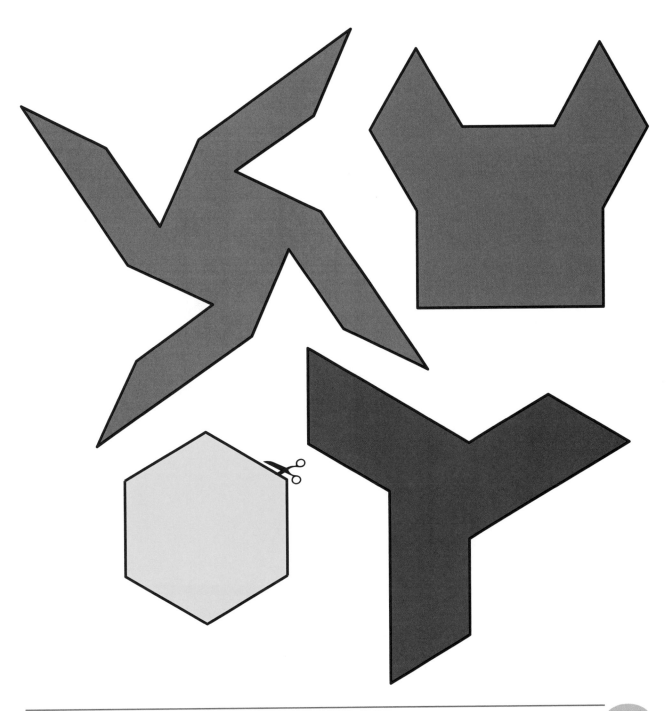

Folding Paper

Dear Family Member:

To complete this page, your child needs a rectangular and a square sheet of paper. Help your child make a square sheet of paper out of a standard rectangular sheet.

Thank you.

Part 1: Use the square sheet of paper.

> Fold a square so that the two halves are alike.

1. How many different ways can you use one fold to get

matching halves? _____

2. How many lines of symmetry are there? _____

Part 2: Use the rectangular sheet of paper that is not a square.

> Fold a rectangle so that the two halves are alike.

1. How many different ways can you use one fold to get

matching halves? _____

2. How many lines of symmetry are there? _____

Symmetry Game

Players

This is a game for two players.

Materials

- pattern blocks
- two sheets like this

Rules

Make a design with six pattern blocks on one side of the line on your sheet. This line will be the line of symmetry for a shape when you are done. Place blocks edge-to-edge. The edge of at least one block must touch the line.

Then switch seats with your partner. Each player must place six blocks on the other side creating a shape with two matching halves.

Slide Design

Make a pattern block quilt design. Use slides to complete the quilt block. Work from Section 1 to 2 to 3 to 4. Trace around the pattern block shapes.

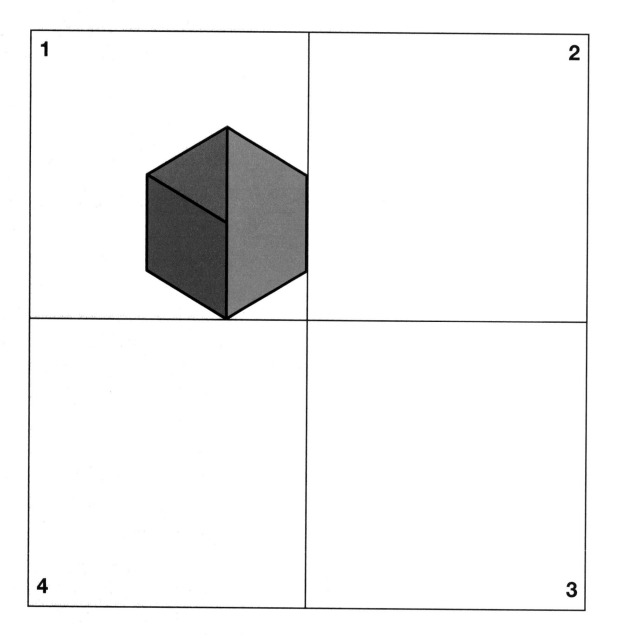

Checked by _____

Name _____ Date _____

Flip Design

Make a pattern block quilt design. Use flips to complete the quilt block. Work from Section 1 to 2 to 3 to 4. Trace around the pattern block shapes.

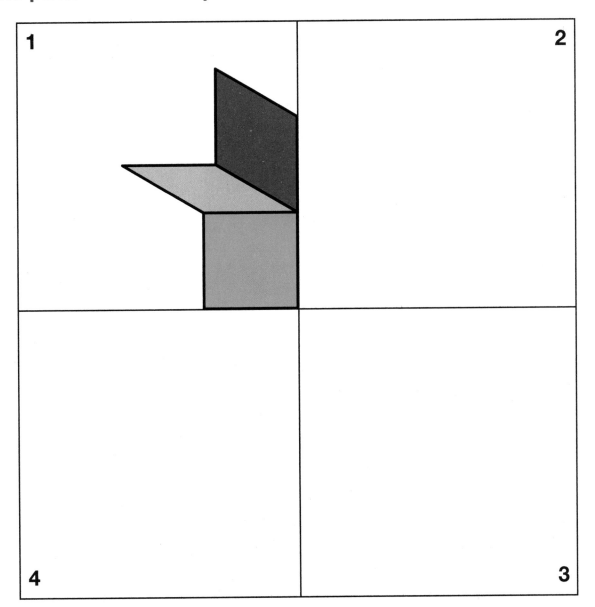

Checked by _____

My Quilt Block Design

I used _____ to complete the design.
(slides or flips)

1	**2**
4	**3**

Checked by _____

Turn Design

Make a pattern block quilt design. Use turns to complete the quilt block. Work from Section 1 to 2 to 3 to 4. Trace around the pattern block shapes.

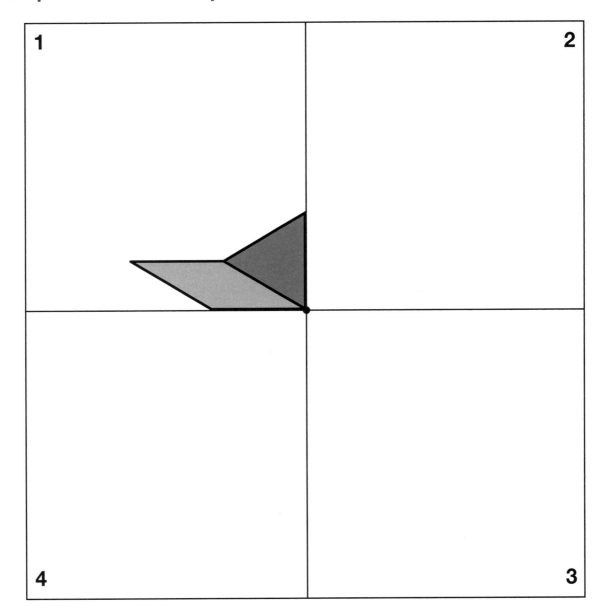

Checked by _____

Slide and Flip

Homework

1. Cut out Set A of the pattern blocks below. Use slides to complete the quilt block. Work from Section 1 to 2 to 3 to 4. Trace around the cut-out shapes.

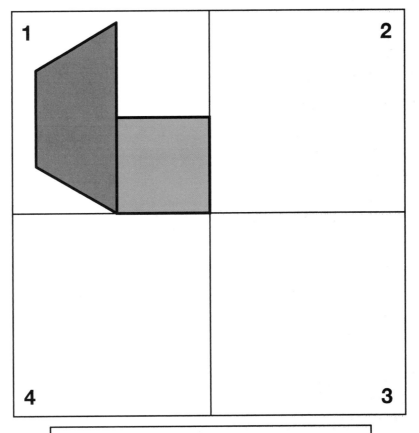

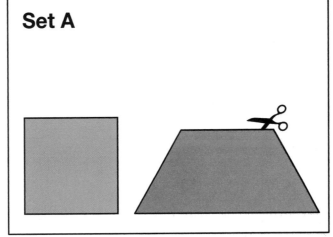

Set A

2. Cut out Set B of the pattern blocks below. Use flips to complete the quilt block. Work from Section 1 to 2 to 3 to 4. Trace around the cut-out shapes.

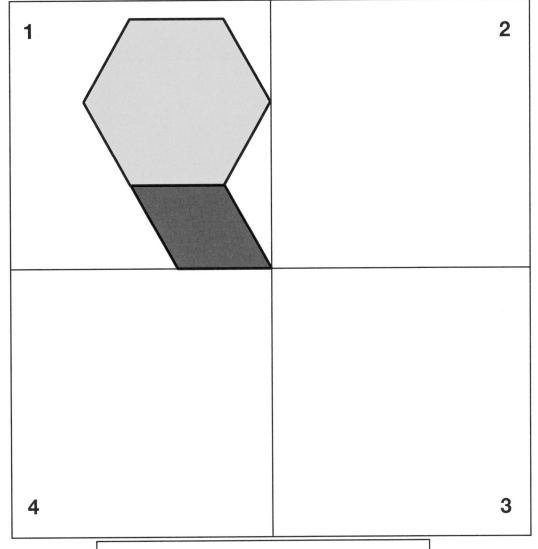

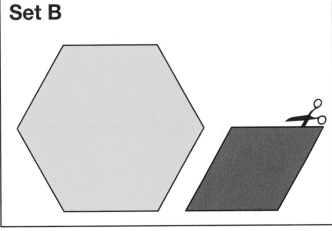

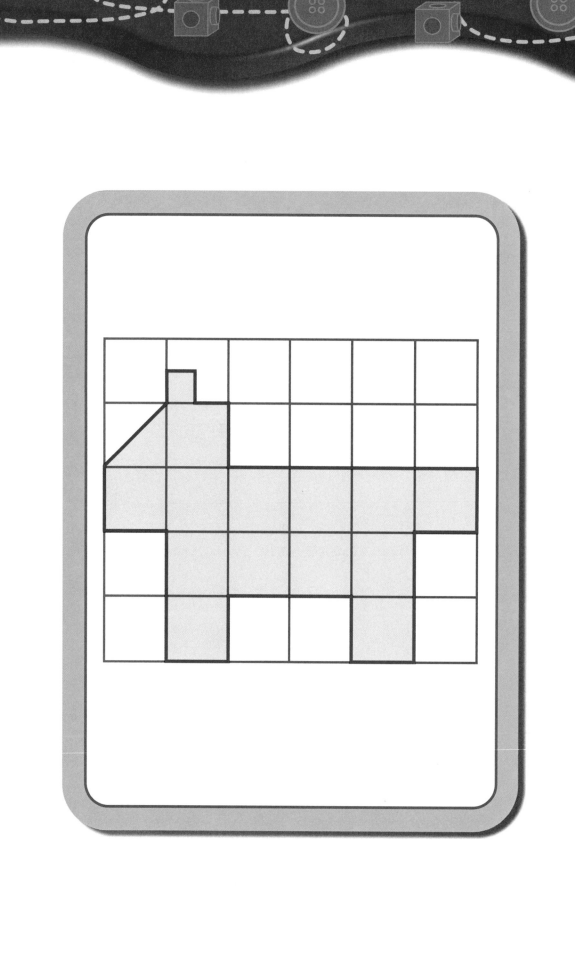

Unit 16

Measuring Area

	Student Guide	Adventure Book	Unit Resource Guide*
Lesson 1			
Introducing Area Measurement	●		
Lesson 2			
Counting Out Areas	●		
Lesson 3			
Length, Width, and Area	●		
Lesson 4			
Area Riddles	●		
Lesson 5			
Area and the Geoboard	●		
Lesson 6			
Grandpa and Willie Tile the Hall		●	

*Unit Resource Guide pages are from the teacher materials.

Area Practice

Find the area of the shapes. Label each shape with its area.

Name _____ Date _____

Finding Area at Home

Find the area of the shapes. Label each shape with its area.

1.

2.

3.

4.

5.

6.

Introducing Area Measurement

Counting Square Centimeters

Find the area of this shape.

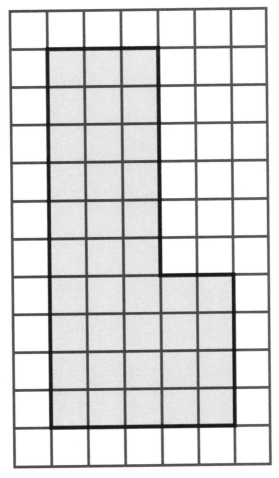

Area = _____ square centimeters

Triangle Flash Cards: Group F Subtraction Facts

- Cut out the flash cards. To practice a subtraction fact, cover the number in the circle. Subtract the two uncovered numbers.

- Divide the cards into three piles: those facts you know and can answer quickly, those you can figure out with a strategy, and those you need to learn.

- Make a list of the facts in the last two piles. These are the facts you need to study.

- Go through all the cards again. This time cover the number in the square.

- Sort the cards into three piles again. Add the facts in the last two piles to your list that you need to study.

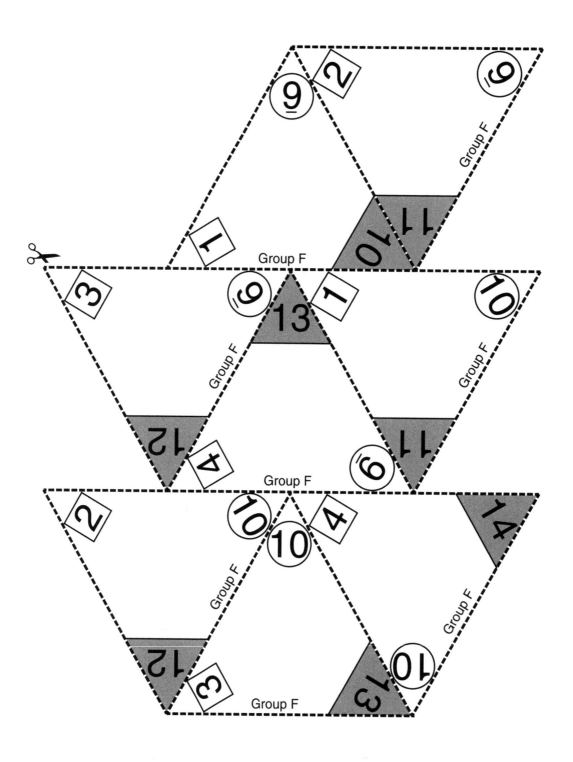

Square Centimeter Fractions

Find the area of each shape.

1.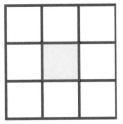

Area = _____

2.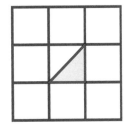

Area = _____

3.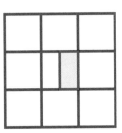

Area = _____

4.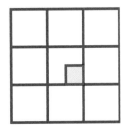

Area = _____

Puzzling Out Halves

Cut out the two $\frac{1}{2}$ square units. Show that these really are each one-half of the whole square unit below. Glue them onto the whole square unit in the work area.

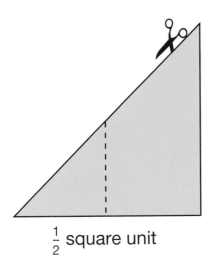

$\frac{1}{2}$ square unit

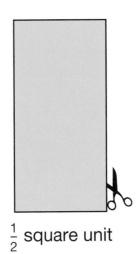

$\frac{1}{2}$ square unit

Work Area

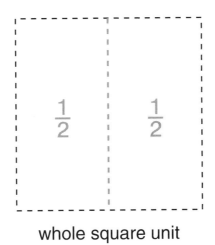

whole square unit

_____ + _____ = _____

Shapes Grid

Find the area covered by each of the shapes shown.

1.

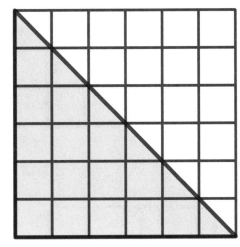

Area = _____ sq cm

2.

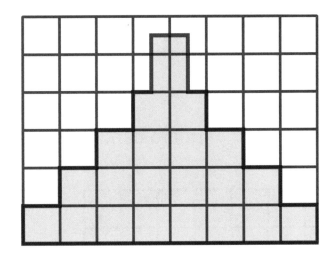

Area = _____ sq cm

3.
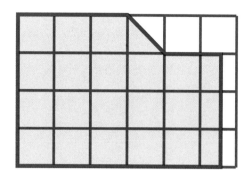

Area = _____ sq cm

4.
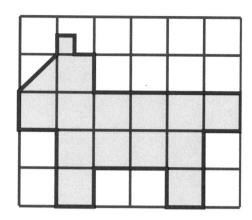

Area = _____ sq cm

5.
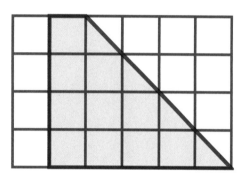

Area = _____ sq cm

6.
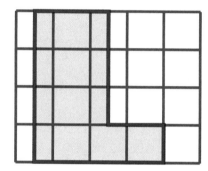

Area = _____ sq cm

7. Draw a shape with an area of $11\frac{1}{2}$ square centimeters on the grid.

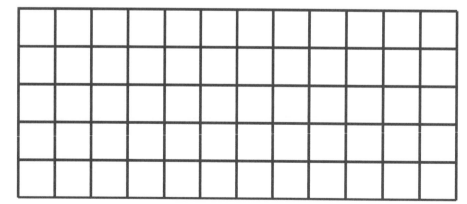

Shapes Grid at Home

Find the area covered by each of the shapes shown.

1.

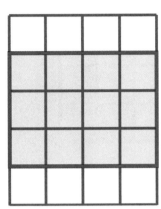

Area = _____ sq cm

2.

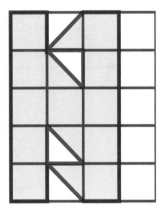

Area = _____ sq cm

3.

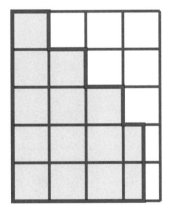

Area = _____ sq cm

4.

Area = _____ sq cm

Name _____   Date _____

5.

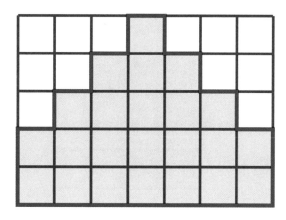

Area = _____ sq cm

6.

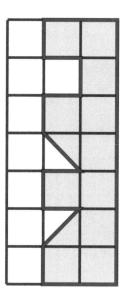

Area = _____ sq cm

7.

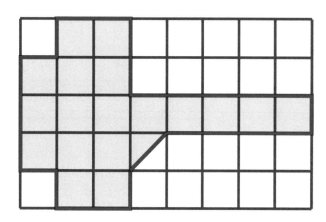

Area = _____ sq cm

8. Draw a shape with an area of $9\frac{1}{4}$ sq centimeters.

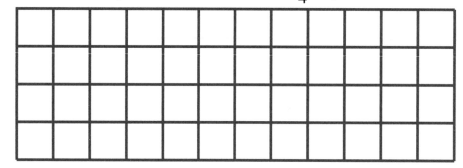

Counting Out Areas

Length, Width, and Area Rectangles

Find the length, width, and area of each of the shapes.

1.

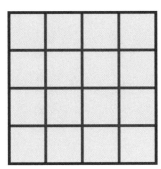

Length = _____ cm

Width = _____ cm

Area   = _____ sq cm

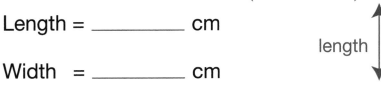

2.

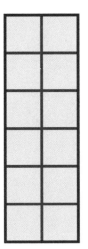

Length = _____ cm

Width = _____ cm

Area   = _____ sq cm

3.

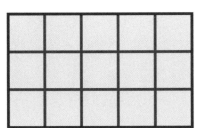

Length = _____ cm

Width = _____ cm

Area   = _____ sq cm

4. Which rectangle has the most area? _____

5. Does it have the largest length or width? _____

6.

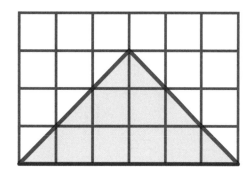

Length = _____ cm

Width = _____ cm

Area   = _____ sq cm

7.

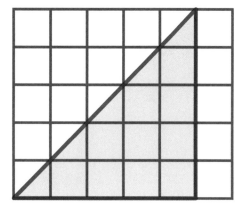

Length = _____ cm

Width = _____ cm

Area   = _____ sq cm

Length, Width, and Area Designs

Find the length, width, and area of each shape.

1.

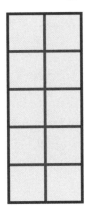

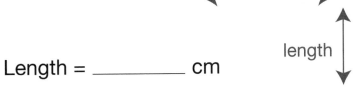

Length = _____ cm

Width = _____ cm

Area   = _____ sq cm

2.

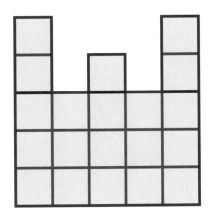

Length = _____ cm

Width = _____ cm

Area   = _____ sq cm

3.

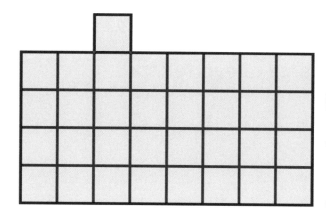

Length = _____ cm

Width = _____ cm

Area   = _____ sq cm

4.

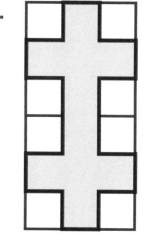

Area   = _____ sq cm

5.

Area   = _____ sq cm

You Make the Shape

1. Draw a rectangle with a length of 3 cm and a width of 6 cm. Label the shape with its area.

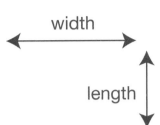

2. Draw a shape with a length of 4 cm, width of 7 cm, and area of 25 sq cm. Is the shape a rectangle? _____

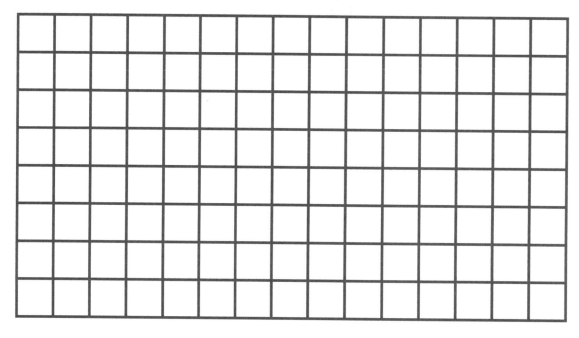

3. Describe a shape of your own. Then draw it on the grid. Include the shape's length, width, and area in your description.

_____

_____

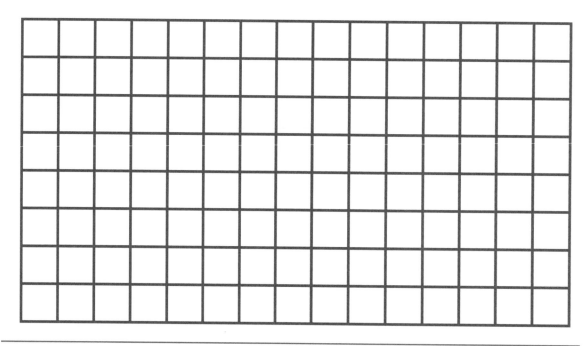

Length, Width, and Area

Area Riddles

For each riddle draw a shape and find its area.

1. My number of ⬜ = 7

   My number of ◺ = 3

   What is my area? _____

2. My number of ▯ = 9

   My number of ▮ = 3

   My number of ◻ = 2

   What is my area? _____

3. My number of ▯ = 6

   My number of ▮ = 4

   My number of ◻ = 1

   What is my area? _____

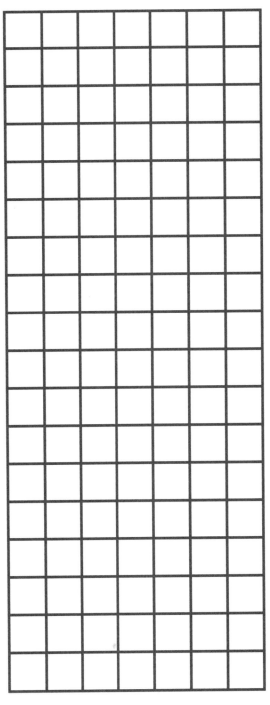

Name _____ Date _____

Area Riddles at Home

1. Count the ▢ , ◺ , ▯ , and ▢ to find the area of this shape.

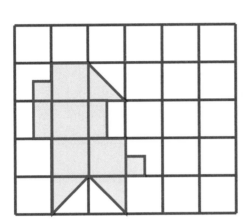

Number of ▢ = _____

Number of ◺ = _____

Number of ▯ = _____

Number of ▢ = _____

Area = _____

2. Draw a shape that fits this riddle. Then find its area.

Number of ▢ = 6

Number of ◺ = 3

Number of ▯ = 2

Number of ▢ = 4

Area = _____

3. Draw a shape that fits this riddle. Then find its area.

Number of = 3

Number of  = 2

Number of ▯ = 2

Number of ▢ = 2

Area = _____

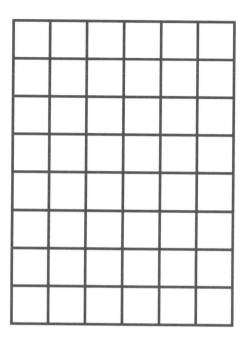

Area Riddles

Area Questions

How are Shapes A and B alike and different?

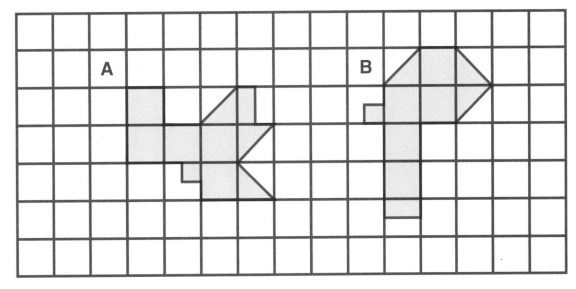

_____

_____

_____

_____

What is the area of Shape A? _____

What is the area of Shape B? _____

Name _____ Date _____

Area Hunt

Make rectangles on your geoboard that match the areas shown. You may not be able to make rectangles for some of the areas. Which areas can you find in more than one way? If you find more than one way, use the geoboards on the following page for the extra shapes.

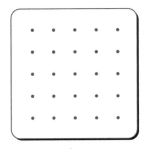

Area = 1 square unit

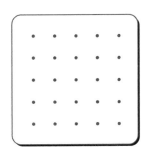

Area = 2 square units

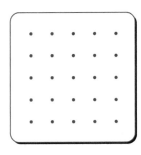

Area = 3 square units

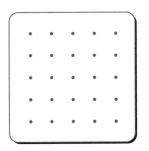

Area = 4 square units

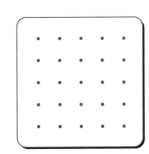

Area = 5 square units

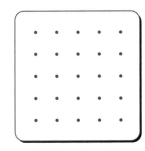

Area = 6 square units

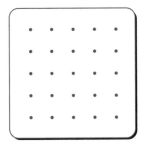

Area = 7 square units

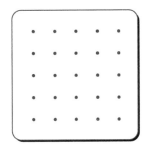

Area = 8 square units

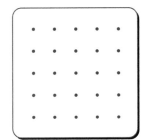

Area = 9 square units

Name _____ Date _____

For extra shapes:

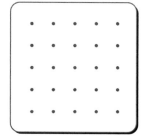

Area = _____

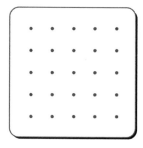

Area = _____

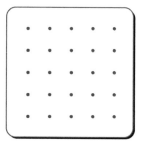

Area = _____

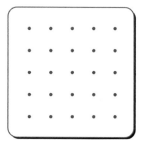

Area = _____

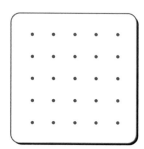

Area = _____

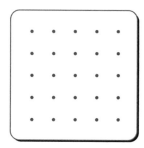

Area = _____

Area and the Geoboard

Geoboard Areas

Make these shapes on the geoboard. Find the area of each shape. Don't forget to write down the units.

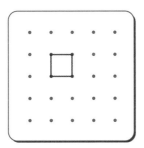

Area = _____

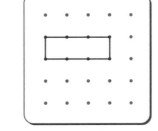

Area = _____

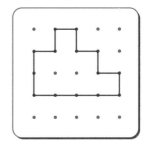

Area = _____

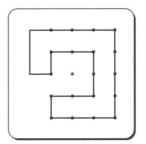

Area = _____

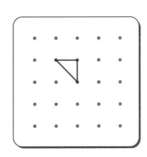

Area = _____

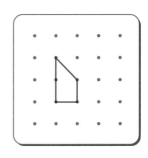

Area = _____

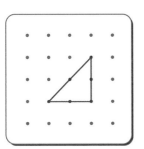

Area = _____

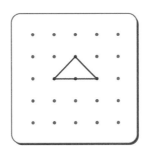

Area = _____

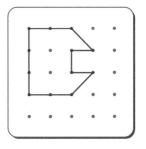

Area = _____

Geoboard Puzzles

Homework

See how many of these geoboard puzzles you can solve on the geoboard. Draw the shapes.

1. A shape with an area of $4\frac{1}{2}$ square units

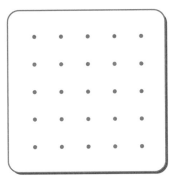

2. A shape with an area of 7 square units

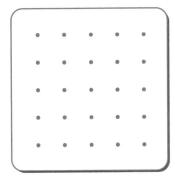

3. A different shape with an area of 7 square units

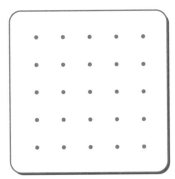

4. A shape with an area of 6 square units that is not a rectangle

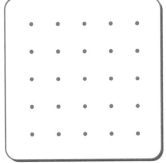

5. A 4-sided figure with an area of 4 square units. Solve this problem in two ways.

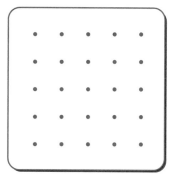 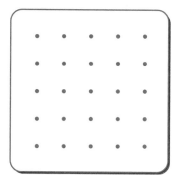

6. A shape with an area of 4 square units that has more than 4 sides

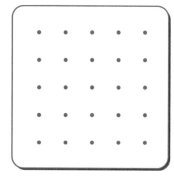

More Geoboard Puzzles

See how many of these geoboard puzzles you can solve on the geoboard. Then draw the shape.

1. A square with an area of 9 square units

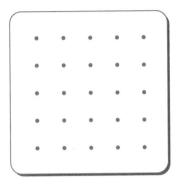

2. A rectangle with an area of 12 square units

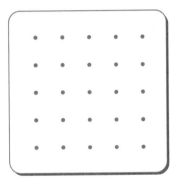

3. A rectangle with an area of 8 square units

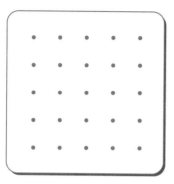

4. A rectangle with an area of 6 square units

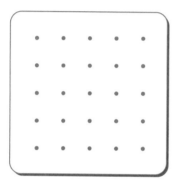

5. A rectangle with an area of 16 square units

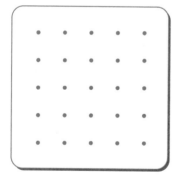

Unit 17

Investigating 3-D Shapes

	Student Guide	Adventure Book	Unit Resource Guide*
Lesson 1			
Exploring 3-D Shapes	●		
Lesson 2			
Sorting 3-D Shapes	●		
Lesson 3			
2-D or Not 2-D	●		●
Lesson 4			
Skeletons of 3-D Shapes	●		
Lesson 5			
Geometry Riddles	●		
Lesson 6			
City of the Future	●		●

Unit Resource Guide pages are from the teacher materials.

Name _____ Date _____

3-D Shape Hunt

Look for these three-dimensional shapes in the classroom.

 sphere

 cube

 cylinder

 rectangular prism

cone

rectangular pyramid

 triangular pyramid

 triangular prism

Record the object and its shape in the data table.

3-D Shape Hunt Data Table

Object	3-D Shape

Exploring 3-D Shapes

Alike and Different

Draw your two 3-D shapes below and label them.

1. How are your two shapes alike?

_____

_____

_____

2. How are your two shapes different?

_____

_____

_____

Name _____ Date _____

3-D Shape Hunt at Home

Dear Family Member:

Your child has been analyzing, describing, and identifying three-dimensional shapes. Help your child find objects at home that have the shapes shown below. Search for as many different examples as possible. The kitchen and your child's play area are good places to look for boxes, balls, cylinders, and cubes. Remind him or her to bring the objects to school. We will use the collection of shapes in class. We will sort the shapes and discuss their similarities and differences.

Thank you for your cooperation.

Search for objects at home that have these three-dimensional shapes. Find as many different shapes as you can.

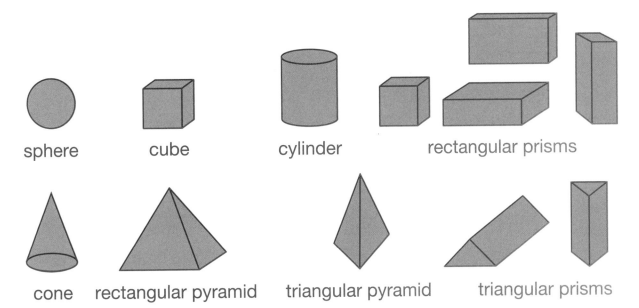

sphere   cube   cylinder   rectangular prisms

cone   rectangular pyramid   triangular pyramid   triangular prisms

Comparing 3-D Shapes

Homework

cone

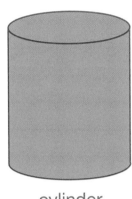

cylinder

1. How are the two shapes alike?

_____

_____

_____

2. How are the two shapes different?

_____

_____

_____

_____

_____

Name _____ Date _____

What Do You Know about This Shape?

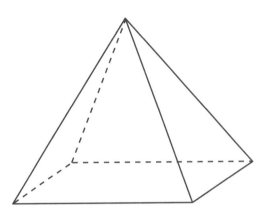 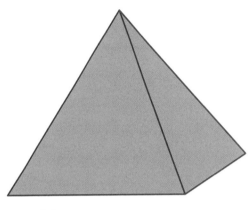

rectangular pyramid

Describe this shape in as many ways as you can.

_____

_____

_____

_____

_____

_____

_____

Triangle Flash Cards: Group G Subtraction Facts

- Cut out the flash cards. To practice a subtraction fact, cover the number in the circle. Subtract the two uncovered numbers.

- Divide the cards into three piles: those facts you know and can answer quickly, those you can figure out with a strategy, and those you need to learn.

- Make a list of the facts in the last two piles. These are the facts you need to study.

- Go through all the cards again. This time cover the number in the square.

- Sort the cards into three piles again. Add the facts in the last two piles to your list that you need to study.

Name ______________________________ Date ________________

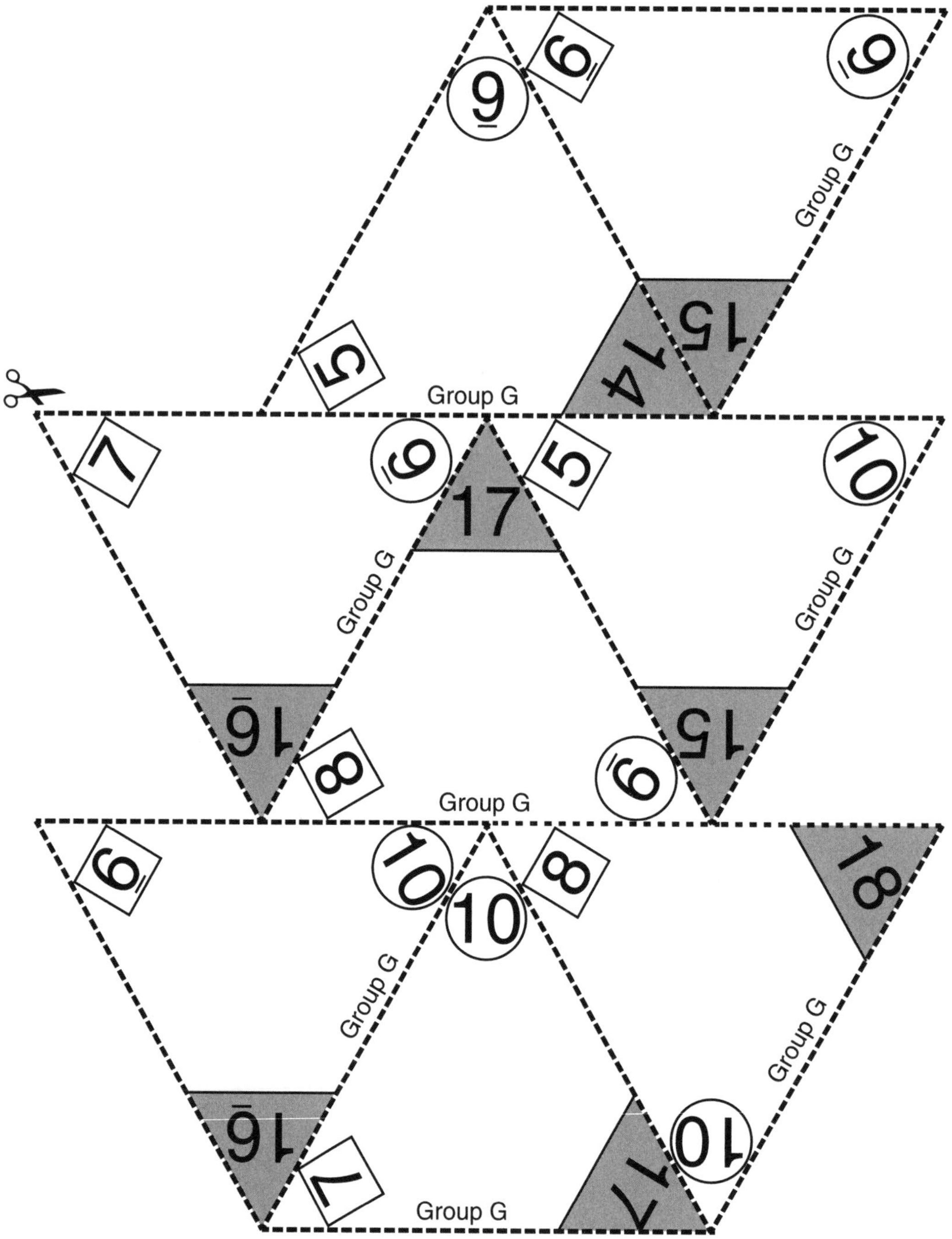

Describing 3-D Shapes

1. What is your 3-D shape? _____

2. Write as many ways as you can think of to describe your shape.

_____

_____

_____

_____

_____

_____

_____

_____

_____

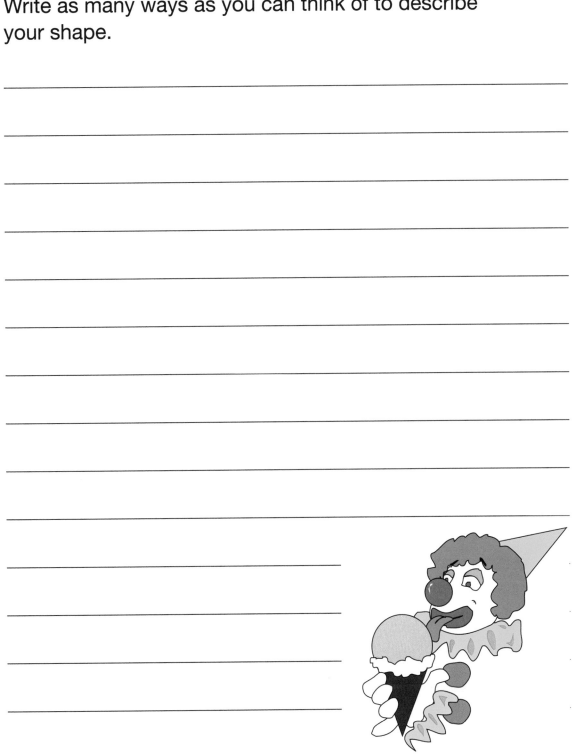

_____

_____

_____

Name _____ Date _____

Sketch 3-D Shapes

Look for three-dimensional shapes at home. In the boxes below, make a sketch of some of the objects. Then tell what shape it has. You may draw more pictures on the back of this paper.

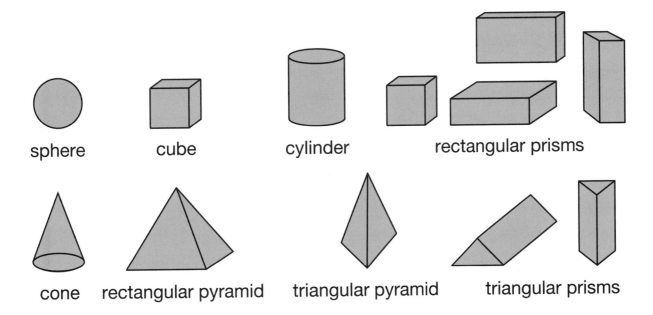

sphere   cube   cylinder   rectangular prisms

cone   rectangular pyramid   triangular pyramid   triangular prisms

1.	2.
Name of object _____	Name of object _____
Shape _____	Shape _____

3.

Name of object _____

Shape _____

4.

Name of object _____

Shape _____

5.

Name of object _____

Shape _____

6.

Name of object _____

Shape _____

Sorting 3-D Shapes

Name _____ Date _____

Sorting 3-D Shapes

Look for pictures of three-dimensional shapes in newspapers and magazines. Cut out the shapes and sort them. Then paste them on a separate sheet of paper in their different groups. Label the groups. On the same piece of paper, write an explanation about how you sorted the shapes.

Dear Family Member:

In class your child compared different three-dimensional shapes by putting these shapes into groups to show their similarities. Maybe the objects in each group had the same shape or the same number of corners. Perhaps one group of shapes could roll and the other group could not. Discuss with your child different ways the shapes he or she cuts out can be grouped. After sorting them, make sure your child pastes the shapes in each group close to one another on a separate piece of paper. Drawing a loop around the shapes that go together may help. Finally, ask your child to label the picture and describe the sorting method.

Thank you.

Name _____ Date _____

3-D Shape Book

Write a story about one of the three-dimensional shapes shown below.

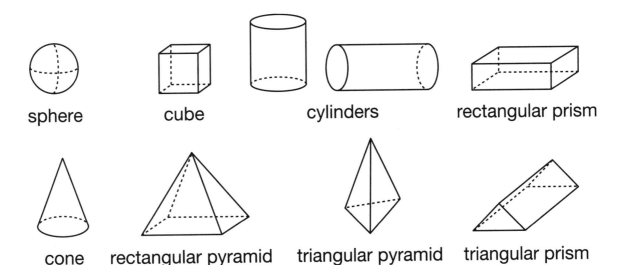

sphere   cube   cylinders   rectangular prism

cone   rectangular pyramid   triangular pyramid   triangular prism

Here are some ideas to help you get started. You may also think of your own idea for a story.

1. A 3-D shape searches for other shapes just like herself.

2. The day I became _____ -shaped.

3. What if everything in the world were shaped like a

    _____

4. A world without _____

Now make a book for your story. Draw pictures on each page.

Edges, Vertices, and Faces

Look at each skeleton of a 3-D shape that you made. How many edges, vertices, and faces does each 3-D shape have? Record the number on the data table.

Skeletons of 3-D Shapes Data Table

Type of Shape	Number of Edges	Number of Vertices (Corners)	Number of Faces (Sides)
cube			
triangular prism			
rectangular pyramid			
triangular pyramid			
rectangular prism			

Faces, Edges, and Vertices

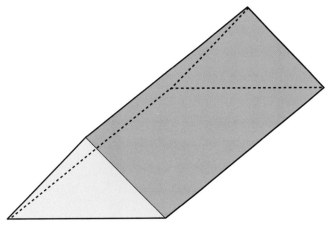

triangular prism

1. How many faces does it have?

_____

2. How many edges does it have?

_____

3. How many vertices does it have?

_____

4. What makes it a triangular prism?

Write Geometry Riddles

Choose a 3-D object from the class collection. Make up a
riddle about the object. Write clues that will help someone
solve your riddle.

_____

_____

_____

_____

_____

_____

- ✂

Here is the answer to my riddle:

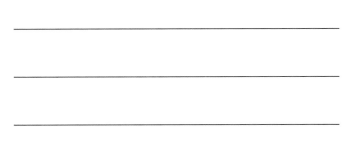 

_____

_____

_____

_____

3-D Shapes around Us

Homework

Look outside for some of the 3-D shapes we studied in class.

Sketch the objects you saw. Then label the 3-D shapes in the picture.

Write about the 3-D shapes on the lines below the picture. What shapes did you see? Were some shapes hard to find?

City of the Future Data Table

How many of each 3-D shape did you use in your city of the future? Record the number in the data table.

City of the Future Data Table

Type of 3-D Shape	Number
cube	
cone	
cylinder	
hemisphere	
rectangular prism	
rectangular pyramid	
sphere	
triangular prism	
triangular pyramid	

Unit 18

Mapping the Rain Forest

	Student Guide	Adventure Book	Unit Resource Guide*
Lesson 1			
Meet Mr. Origin and Mr. Origin's Map	●		
Lesson 2			
Mapping Our World	●		
Lesson 3			
Rain Forest Trails	●		●
Lesson 4			
Mr. Origin Left/Right or Front/Back	●		
Lesson 5			
Lords of the River: The Giant Otter		●	

Unit Resource Guide pages are from the teacher materials.

Mr. Origin's Data Table

Look at Mr. Origin's Map. Tell where each shape is.

Shape	Distance (in ___cm___)	Direction
triangle ▼	7	R
square ◆		
rhombus ◆		
hexagon ⬡		

Meet Mr. Origin and Mr. Origin's Map

Name _____ Date _____

Meet Mr. Origin and Ms. Origin

Dear Family Member:

In class today, we used a plastic figure called Mr. Origin to help develop skills in understanding the directions right/left and front/back. Please have your child read aloud the *Meet Mr. Origin and Ms. Origin* Homework Pages. As you listen to the descriptions accompanying the pictures, ask your child to pause whenever he or she reads a question contained in the text. You and your child can take turns answering the questions.

Thank you for your help.

Read aloud *Meet Mr. Origin and Ms. Origin* to a family member.

Parent's Signature _____

Child's Signature _____

Return this sheet to school by _____

This is Mr. Origin.

This is Ms. Origin.

Mr. and Ms. Origin help us learn about directions and distance.

They have mittens on their right hands. That helps us tell right and left.

The buttons tell us this is their front side.

In this picture, the cup is to Ms. Origin's right.

The other side is called their "back."

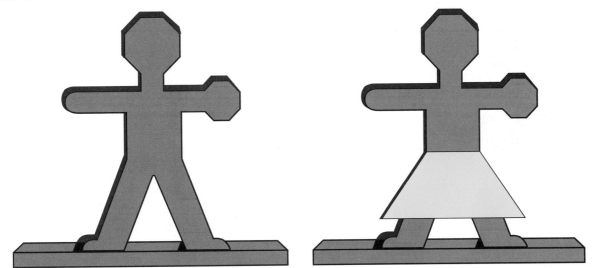

What did you see on their front that is missing on their back? When you look at them turned this way, your right hand is on the same side as theirs.

Ms. Origin's back is toward us.

Now the cup is to Ms. Origin's left.

Mr. Origin is standing on his head.
Is the mouse in the cup to Mr. Origin's right or left?
You are to Mr. Origin's back.

Where Are They?

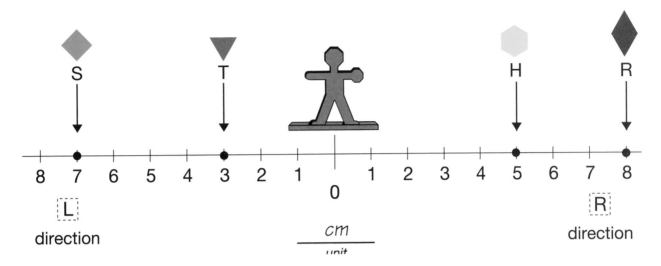

1. How far and in what direction is the triangle from Mr. Origin?

   _____   _____
   Distance   Direction

2. Where is the blue rhombus? _____ _____
                                Distance   Direction

3. What is the distance between the blue rhombus and

   the hexagon? _____

4. Distance between triangle and square? _____

5. Distance between triangle and hexagon? _____

6. Distance between the triangle and blue rhombus? _____

7. Distance between the square and hexagon? _____

Ada's Kitchen

- Daryl visited Ada's house. He saw that there were six chairs around her kitchen table.

- Daryl found the dog dish when he accidentally stepped into it. The dog dish was in front of the stove.

- The stove and refrigerator were next to each other. They were along the same wall as the sink.

- The windowsill took up about half of the right wall.

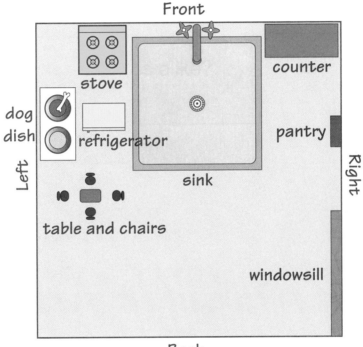

Daryl's Map

 **Discuss**

1. Does Daryl's map match what he saw in the kitchen? Explain.

2. Compare the sizes of the objects. Does the map seem right? What would you change about Daryl's map?

Meter Square

Below is a picture of a square on the floor. In the square are two paste jars, a math book, one rubber band, one calculator, one Mr. Origin, two pencils, and two cups.

Work in groups. Make a square on the floor as shown in the picture. Then place the other objects on the floor as they appear in the picture.

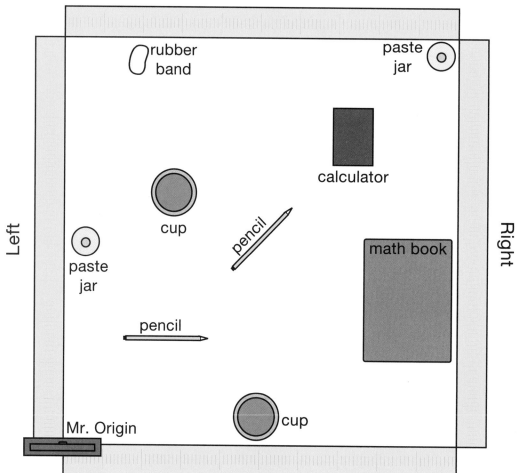

Name _____ Date _____

Classroom Map

Work with your group. Discuss the size and location of various objects in your classroom. Then work alone to make a list of the objects you will include in your map. When drawing your map:

- Put objects in the **right place** compared to one another.
- Try to make the objects the **right size**.
- Label the objects that you draw.
- When you are finished, compare your map with the maps your group members created.
- Place Mr. Origin at the back corner on the left.

List the objects you plan to include on your classroom map.

1. _____Mr. Origin_____

2. __Classroom door__

3. _____

4. _____

5. _____

6. _____

7. _____

8. _____

Name _____ Date _____

Answer the following questions:

1. Is the teacher's desk bigger or smaller than the other desks?

   _____

2. Tell which objects are located in the . . .

   A. Front of the room _____

   B. Back of the room _____

   C. Middle of the room _____

   D. Right side of the room _____

   E. Left side of the room _____

   _____

   _____

   _____

   _____

Name _____ Date _____

My Classroom Map

Front

Left

Right

Back

My Room at Home Map

Make a map of a room at home. Use the next page if the map is the right shape. If it is not the right shape, draw the shape of your room on another sheet of paper. Be sure to place the objects in your map in the **right position.** Also, try to make them the **right size.**

List the objects to include on your map.

1. _____ 2. _____

3. _____ 4. _____

5. _____ 6. _____

7. _____ 8. _____

Answer the following questions:

1. What object is closest to the door?

    _____

2. What is in the middle of the room?

    _____

3. What is the longest object in the room?

    _____

My Room at Home Map

How to Make Rain Forest Trails

This is how you make your rain forest animals.

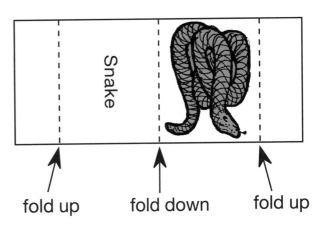

fold up   fold down   fold up

Make sure there is at least one animal in every direction from Mr. Origin.

Tape the parrot and the snake to Mr. Origin's right.

Tape the turtle to Mr. Origin's left.

Place the animals crosswise on the axes trails.

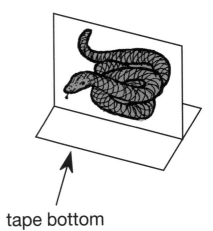

tape bottom

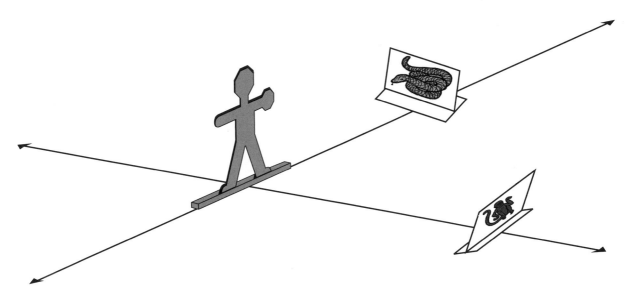

Rain Forest Trails Data Table

Record the distance and direction of your rain forest animals in the data table.

Rain Forest Trails Data Table
Mr. Origin Setup # _____

Animal	Distance (in _____) *unit*	Direction
armadillo		
spider monkey		
howler monkey		
parrot		R
turtle		L
snake		R

Mr. Origin Left/Right or Front/Back

Draw a picture of your lab setup. Be sure to label the axes left, right, front, and back.

Collect

Work with your group to fill in the data table.

Mr. Origin Left/Right or Front/Back Data Table
Mr. Origin Setup # _____
Group # _____

Animal	Distance (in _____) _{unit}	Direction
armadillo		
spider monkey		
howler monkey		
parrot		
turtle		
snake		

Name _____ Date _____

Map

Look at the data table. Decide as a group how to number the lines on the map. Then plot the animals on the map.

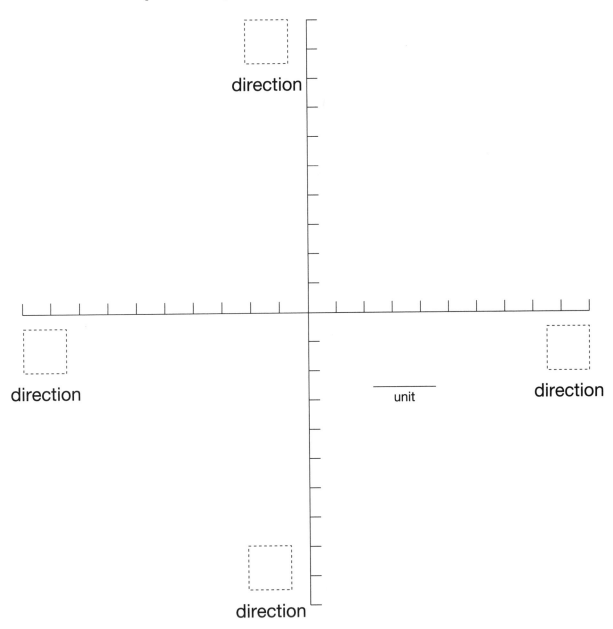

direction

direction

unit

direction

direction

Name _____   Date _____

1. A. Use your map or data table. Predict how far the parrot is from the turtle.

    _____

    B. How did you find the answer? _____

    C. Measure the distance from the parrot to the turtle. Is your answer the same as your prediction?

    _____

2. A. What animal is the farthest from the front of Mr. Origin?

    _____

    B. How far from his front is it? _____

3. A. What animal is the farthest from the back of Mr. Origin?

    _____

    B. How far from his back is it? _____

4. What is the distance between these two animals?

    _____

5. How far is the turtle from the snake?

    _____

Changing Directions

Yoko has a small Mr. Origin on her desk. She uses two rulers to measure distances, one to the right and one to the left. Remember that Mr. Origin has a mitten on his right hand.

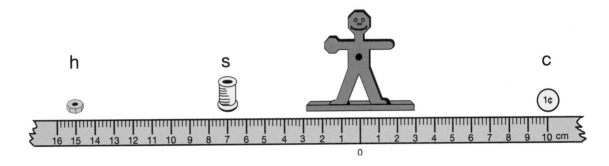

Mark the location of the coin (c), the spool (s), and the hex nut (h) on the line.

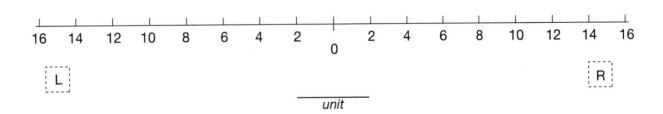

unit

Name _____ Date _____

Mr. Origin Map and Data Tables

Part 1

Here is Mr. Origin in a park. There is a front/back line and a right/left line. Fill in the data table.

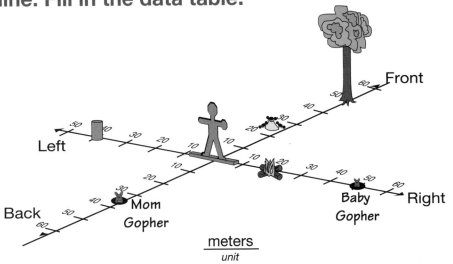

Mr. Origin in the Park Data Table

Object	Distance (in _____) unit	Direction
can		
campfire		
anthill		
oak tree		
baby gopher		

Name _____ Date _____

1. Baby gopher is lost. Tell the mother gopher how to get to him.

   _____

   _____

2. How far is the tree from the anthill? _____

3. How far is it from the campfire to the can? _____

4. How could you travel from the campfire to the anthill?

   _____

   _____

Part 2

Ivana has a Mr. Origin on her desk. She uses a ruler to measure distances. Here is her data table.

Ivana's Data Table

Object	Distance (in ___cm___) unit	Direction
A. Marble	8 cm	R
B. Penny	8 cm	L
C. Washer	5 cm	R

Name _____ Date _____

Draw the marble, penny, and washer on the map below.

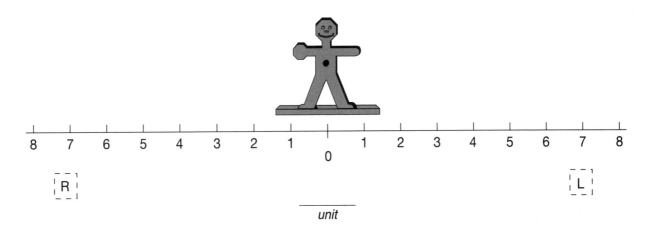

1. How far is the marble from the washer? _____

2. How far is the penny from the marble? _____

3. How far is the penny from the washer? _____

4. Which object is closest to Mr. Origin? _____

5. Which object is farthest from Mr. Origin? _____

6. Which object is the farthest to the right? _____

7. Which object is the farthest to the left? _____

Unit 19

Patterns in Data

	Student Guide	Adventure Book	Unit Resource Guide*
Lesson 1			
Armadillo Families		⬤	
Lesson 2			
Counting Kids	⬤		
Lesson 3			
Function Machines	⬤		⬤
Lesson 4			
Gzorp	⬤		

Unit Resource Guide pages are from the teacher materials.

Name _____ Date _____

Counting Kids at Home

Homework

| The _____ family
Number of kids in my family including me:

_____ | |
Name	Age
1.	
2.	
3.	
4.	
5.	
6.	
7.	
8.	
9.	
10.	
Parent Initial ☐	

Counting Kids

Counting Kids

Draw a picture of the survey. Show what information you are looking for. Show how you might find it.

I predict that the most common number of kids is _____.

Counting Kids Data Table

Number of _____	Number of _____		Total
	Tallies		
1			
2			
3			
4			
5			
6			
7			
8			
9			
10			
11			
		Total Number of Families	

Make a bar graph of your data on graph paper. Label the axes, and number the lines. Then fill in the bars.

Work with a partner to answer Questions 1–7.

1. What is the total number of families? _____

2. What is half of the total number of families? _____

3. How many families have more than 3 kids? _____

4. **A.** How many families have three or more kids?

    _____

    B. Is this more or fewer than half of all the families?

    _____

5. **A.** How many families have fewer than three kids?

    _____

    B. Is this more or fewer than half of all the families?

    _____

6. What is the range of the number of kids?

_____ to _____

(This is the smallest to the largest number.)

7. What number of kids occurs most often? _____

(This is the most common number of kids in a family.)

8. Compare your family with the other families in your class.

   A. How many kids are in your family? _____

   B. How many families have more kids than yours?

   _____

   C. How many other families have the same number of kids as yours?

   _____

   D. How many families have fewer kids than yours?

   _____

9. Does your family have more, fewer, or the same number of kids than the most common number of kids found in the survey?

_____

Name _____ Date _____

Cody and Derek Count Kids

Cody and Derek made a graph of their *Counting Kids* data.

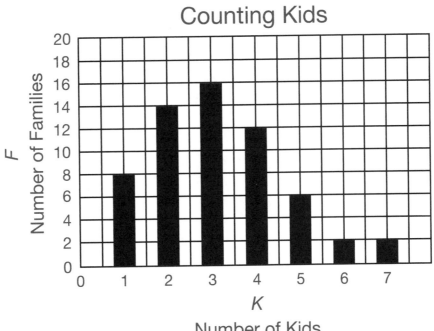

1. What is the most common number of kids in a family? _____

2. How many families have five or more kids? _____

3. How many families have fewer than three kids? _____

4. What is the range of number of kids in the class's families?

   _____ to _____

5. How many families were included in the survey? _____

Name _____   Date _____

Comparing Graphs

Kathy and Andy attend different schools. Information about their classes is shown in the graphs below.

Andy's Class

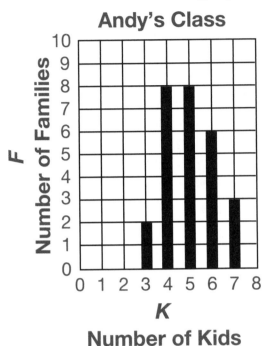

Kathy's Class

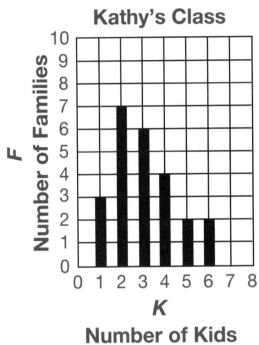

1. What is the most common number of kids in a family in Andy's class?

   _____

2. **A.** How many families in Kathy's class have three or fewer kids?

   _____

   B. Is this more or less than half the families? Explain.

   _____

3. **A.** Which class has more families? _____

   B. How many more families?

   _____

   C. Explain how you found your answer. _____

   _____

   _____

4. Does your class's graph look more like Andy's Class or Kathy's Class? Tell how they are alike.

   _____

   _____

   _____

   _____

   _____

Counting Kids

Doubling Machine and Input-Output Data Table

Complete the table for the Doubling Machine.

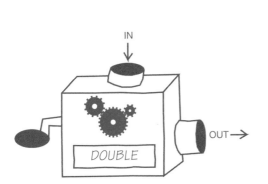

Input-Output Data Table

Input	Output
12	
5	
24	
17	
43	
31	

Use your calculator as a doubling machine. Double the numbers in the table. Does your calculator give the same answers that you did?

Target Numbers—Finding Half

Work with a partner. Use Rosa and Scottie's guess-and-check method to find half of the target number.

Target
Number
136

Input	Output	Next Guess – *Higher or Lower*

Target
Number
278

Input	Output	Next Guess – *Higher or Lower*

Function Machines

What's My Rule?

Players

This is a game for two players.

Materials

- paper and pencil
- a copy of *Function Machine Data Tables*

Rules

1. The first player thinks of a rule for changing numbers.

2. The player writes the rule down on another sheet of paper but does not show the rule to the other player.

3. The second player gives input numbers to the first player.

4. The first player uses the rule to get the output number.

5. The input and output numbers are written on a Function Machine data table.

6. The second player tries to guess the rule.

7. When the second player guesses the rule, the first player writes it in the box above each table.

Rule:

The input number is 15.

Then the output is 17. What's my rule?

Input	Output
4	6
10	12
15	17

Take turns making up rules and guessing.

Halves and Doubles

Complete these tables for the Doubling Machine.

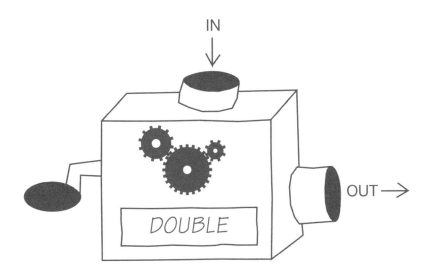

Input	Output
3	
	12
15	
	36
19	
	80

Input	Output
8	
	20
14	
50	
70	
	200

Name _____   Date _____

Function Machines

Fill out the tables for these Function Machines.

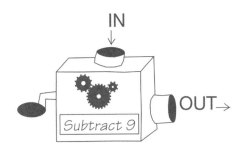

Rule: Rule:

Subtract 9	

Input	Output
9	
11	
13	
	5
	7
18	
21	
25	

Input	Output
1	7
3	9
5	11
	14
	15
	18
14	
20	

Input-Output

Complete these tables for the two Function Machines. The rule is given for the first table. Find the rule for the second table.

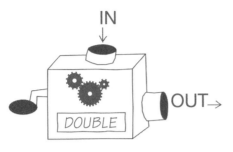

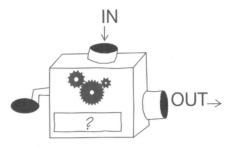

Rule:

Double

Input	Output
3	
8	
	18
23	
	70
125	

Rule:

Input	Output
5	14
7	16
8	17
	18
	20
21	

L-Gator

The L-Gator is only one square when it is one year old.

 one-year-old L-Gator

It has no teeth at first. By the second year it grows two teeth.

 two-year-old L-Gator

1. How many squares does an L-Gator have when it is two

    years old? _____

By the third year, the L-Gator looks a little dangerous.

 three-year-old L-Gator

2. How many teeth does a three-year-old L-Gator have?

    _____

3. How many squares does a three-year-old L-Gator have?

    _____

4. How many teeth does an L-Gator grow each year?

    _____

5. Without drawing a five-year-old L-Gator, could you tell how many teeth and squares it would have? _____

6. How can you find out? _____

_____

7. How old is the L-Gator below? _____

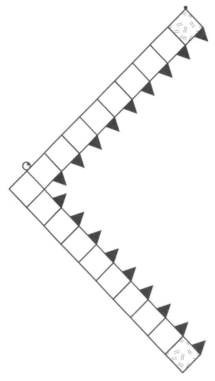

8. How old would an L-Gator be if it had 21 squares? _____

9. How old would an L-Gator be if it had 51 squares? _____

10. How can you find out how many teeth and squares a 100-year-old L-Gator would have? _____

_____

Three-Winged Blue Bird

The Three-Winged Blue Bird has four squares when it is one year old.

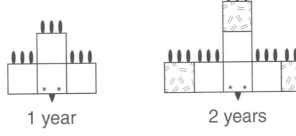

1 year   2 years

1. How many squares does it have when it is two years old?

   _____

2. How many squares does a Three-Winged Blue Bird grow

   each year? _____

3. Draw a five-year-old Three-Winged Blue Bird.

4. How many squares does a ten-year-old Three-Winged Blue

Bird have? _____ Show your work.

5. How old is a Three-Winged Blue Bird with 40 squares?

_____ Show your work.

Double Worm

This is how a One-Eyed Double Worm looks when it is born.

 At birth

The next year, the One-Eyed Double Worm is twice as large.

 1 year

The year after that, it doubles in length again.

 2 years

It keeps on growing, getting twice as large every year.

 3 years

1. Do you think a One-Eyed Double Worm as old as you would

   be very big? _____ Explain. _____

   _____

   _____

2. How long would an eight-year-old One-Eyed Double Worm be?

   _____ Show your work.

3. Would you like to meet a One-Eyed Double Worm that is

   50 years old? _____ Explain. _____

   _____

   _____

There are many kinds of Double Worms on Gzorp. All the different kinds of Double Worms grow twice as long every year. Double Worms always grow in a straight line. Here is a Three-Eyed Double Worm at birth.

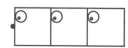

4. Draw a picture of the Three-Eyed Double Worm when it is one year old.

5. How many squares will it have when it is four years old?

   _____ Show your work.

6. How old is a Three-Eyed Double Worm with 96 squares?

   _____ Show your work.

7. How many squares will it have when it is six years old?

   _____ Show your work.

Three-Eyed Exopus

Homework

The Three-Eyed Exopus has five squares when it is one year old. It has nine squares when it is two years old.

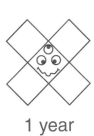
1 year

2 years

1. How many squares does it grow each year? _____

2. Draw a four-year-old Three-Eyed Exopus.

3. How many squares does a ten-year-old Three-Eyed Exopus have? _____ Show your work.

4. How old is a Three-Eyed Exopus with 33 squares?

_____ Show your work.

Berry Drink

For one serving:

¼ cup fresh strawberries

⅓ cup white grape juice

¼ cup raspberry sherbet

¼ teaspoon lemon juice

3 ice cubes (optional)

Mix all ingredients in a blender.

Unit 20

Putting Fractions to Use

	Student Guide	Adventure Book	Unit Resource Guide*
Lesson 1			
Useful Fractions	●		
Lesson 2			
Classroom Fractions	●		
Lesson 3			
Geoboard Fractions	●		
Lesson 4			
End-of-Year Test			●

Unit Resource Guide pages are from the teacher materials.

How Many Inches?

Measure the following distances to the nearest $\frac{1}{4}$ inch. First, each partner makes a measurement. If your measurements differ, measure again. Then decide on a correct measurement.

Object	Kind of Measure-ment	Partner 1's Measure-ment (in inches)	Partner 2's Measure-ment (in inches)	Agreed Measure-ment (in inches)
one person's thumb	length			
scissors	length			
this paper	length			
	width			
one person's foot	length			
math book	perimeter			
student desk	width			

Name _____ Date _____

Inch Questions

1. How long is the chalk? _____

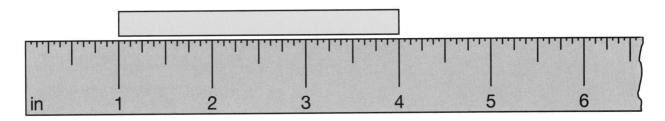

2. How long is this eraser? _____

Alexander
Eraser Company

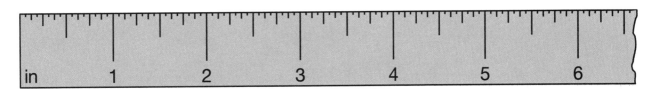

3. How long is the pencil? _____

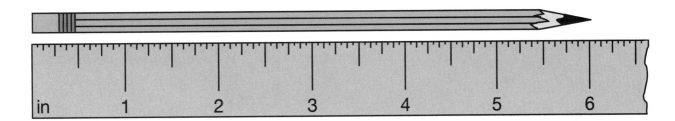

4. If you sharpened the pencil so that it becomes $1\frac{1}{2}$ inches shorter than it is now, how long would it be?

_____

5. Maria is making a train with three pieces of chalk. One piece is 2 inches long; the second piece is $1\frac{1}{2}$ inches long; the last piece is $2\frac{1}{2}$ inches long. How long is the train?

_____

Useful Fractions

Name _____ Date _____

Berry Drink

Use the one-serving recipe to make two- and three-serving recipes.

Berry Drink

For one serving:

$\frac{1}{4}$ cup fresh strawberries

$\frac{1}{3}$ cup white grape juice

$\frac{1}{4}$ cup raspberry sherbet

$\frac{1}{4}$ teaspoon lemon juice

3 ice cubes (optional)

Mix all ingredients in a blender.

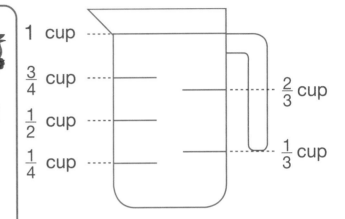

1 cup

$\frac{3}{4}$ cup

$\frac{1}{2}$ cup

$\frac{1}{4}$ cup

$\frac{2}{3}$ cup

$\frac{1}{3}$ cup

Berry Drink

For two servings:

_____ fresh strawberries

_____ white grape juice

_____ raspberry sherbet

_____ lemon juice

_____ ice cubes

Berry Drink

For three servings:

_____ fresh strawberries

_____ white grape juice

_____ raspberry sherbet

_____ lemon juice

_____ ice cubes

Name _____ Date _____

More Function Machines

Fill out the tables for these function machines.

1.
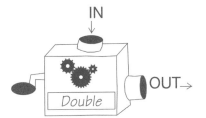

2.
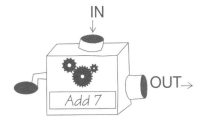

Input	Output
1	
$\frac{1}{4}$	
15	
	18
	24
	38
$\frac{1}{2}$	
	9

Input	Output
1	
2	
5	
	13
	29
	15
94	
	7

Name _____   Date _____

3.

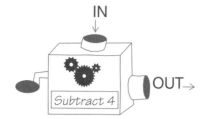

Input	Output
11	
9	
15	
	18
	24
	38
4	
	9

4.

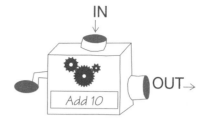

Input	Output
1	
2	
5	
	13
	29
	35
94	
	27

Useful Fractions

Nailing It Down

1. Mr. Robinson, the carpenter, needs help sorting his nails. This is a life-size picture of the nails. How long is each nail in inches? (Measure to the nearest quarter inch.)

A. _____

B. _____

C. _____

D. _____

2. Grandpa and Willie are repairing a fence. They need a board that is 36 inches long. They have only a 12-inch ruler. How many times does Grandpa need to use the ruler? Explain how you found your answer.

_____

_____

_____

_____

_____

Fraction Trains

Use connecting cubes to answer each question. Draw pictures of the connecting cubes for each problem.

1. Make a train with 3 green and 1 red connecting cubes.

    A. What fraction of the train is green? _____

    B. What fraction of the train is red? _____

2. Make a train with 3 blue and 3 white connecting cubes.

    A. What fraction of the train is blue? _____

    B. What fraction of the train is white? _____

    C. What other fraction shows what part is white? _____

3. Make a train of 5 connecting cubes that is $\frac{3}{5}$ blue and the rest is red.

   A. How many connecting cubes are blue? _____

   B. How many connecting cubes are white? _____

   C. What fraction of the train is red? _____

4. Make a train with 3 green, 3 blue, 3 white, and 3 red connecting cubes.

   A. What fraction of the train is green? _____

   B. What fraction is blue? _____

   C. What fraction is not white? _____

   What is another name for this fraction? _____

   D. Choose a part of this train. Write a fraction for your part. If possible, write a different fraction for your part.

   _____

Classroom Fractions

Name _____ Date _____

Fraction Problems

Draw pictures and write the fractions for your answers to these problems.

1. Christina looked outside her window and saw 4 birds. Two of the birds were blue and 2 were white. What fraction of the birds were blue?

2. Justin set the table for dinner. He put 8 cups on the table. There were 2 blue cups, 2 green cups, 2 pink cups, and 2 yellow cups.

   A. What fraction of the cups were blue? _____

   B. What fraction of the cups were green? _____

   C. What fraction of the cups were pink? _____

   D. What fraction of the cups were not yellow? _____

3. Cecelia had 4 marbles in her pocket. One was metal and 3 were glass. What fraction of the marbles were metal? What fraction of the marbles were glass?

4. Jorge took 6 books out of the library. There were 4 science fiction books and 2 animal stories. What fraction of the books were science fiction? What fraction of the books were animal stories?

5. Rachel counted how many cars went past her window one afternoon. She counted 5 cars. If two of the cars were gray, what fraction was gray? Make up another fraction that fits your picture.

Classroom Fractions

Fraction Circles

There are 4 circles below. Color the circles to show $\frac{3}{4}$.

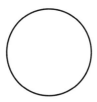 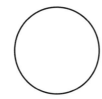 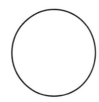 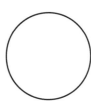

What did you do to show $\frac{3}{4}$? _____

_____

Explain how you know your picture is correct.

_____

_____

_____

_____

_____

_____

Geoboard Halves

Work with a partner. Make this rectangle on your geoboard.

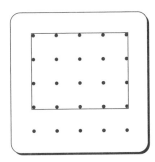

How many ways can you find to divide this rectangle into halves? Record each way you find below.

Name _____   Date _____

May the Fourths Be with You

Homework

1. Draw circles around the pictures that show fourths.

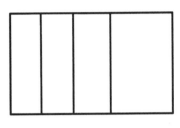  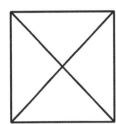

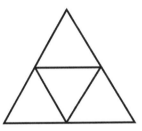 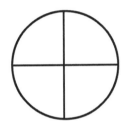 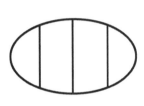

2. Put a large X on the pictures that show $\frac{1}{4}$.

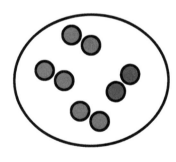 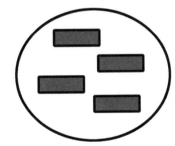 

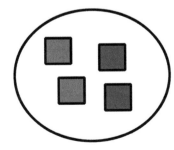 

3. Sal has 3 quarters. What fraction of a dollar does she have? How many cents does she have?

_____

_____

_____

4. Four students have some quarters. Tyrone has $\frac{1}{4}$ of a dollar. Ann has $\frac{3}{4}$ of a dollar. Henry has $\frac{2}{4}$ of a dollar. Lin has $\frac{2}{4}$ of a dollar. How many quarters do they have altogether? How much money do they have altogether? (Draw pictures or use quarters to help you solve the problem.)

_____

_____

_____

Grade 2

Glossary

This glossary provides definitions or examples of key terms in the Grade 2 lessons as a resource for students and parents. See the Glossary in the *Teacher Implementation Guide* for more detailed definitions.

A

Area (Unit 16)
The amount of space a shape covers. Area is measured in square units.

B

Base-ten Pieces (Unit 6)
A set of blocks that students use to represent numbers. A skinny is made of 10 bits and a flat is made of 100 bits.

Nickname	Picture
bit	
skinny	
flat	

Bit (Unit 6)
The smallest of the base-ten pieces. It often represents 1. (See also base-ten pieces.)

C

Centimeter (Unit 5)
A unit of length in the metric system. A centimeter (cm) is 1/100 of a meter. This rectangle is one centimeter long.

Cone (Unit 17)
A type of three-dimensional shape. Examples:

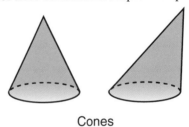

Cones

Corner (Unit 15)
A corner is the point where two sides or edges of a shape meet. Also called a vertex.

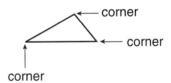

Cube (Unit 17)
A three-dimensional shape with six square faces that are all the same size.

Cube Model (Unit 7)
A shape made with connecting cubes.

Cube Model Plan (Unit 7)
A grid that shows how to build a cube model. The number in each square shows the number of cubes stacked over that square.

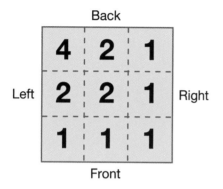

See the picture of the cube model for this plan under Cube Model.

Cubic Centimeter (Unit 10)
The volume of a cube that is one centimeter long on each edge.

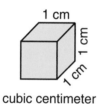

cubic centimeter

Cubit (Unit 4)
A very old unit of length. It is the distance from the elbow to the tip of the longest finger.

Cylinder (Unit 15)
A type of three-dimensional shape. Examples:

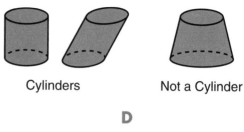

Cylinders   Not a Cylinder

D

E

Edge (Unit 17)
A line where two faces of a three-dimensional shape meet.

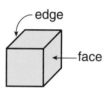

Equal-arm Balance (Unit 8)
See two-pan balance

Estimate (Unit 4)
1. (adjective) a number that is close to the desired number
2. (verb) to approximate

Even Number (Unit 2)
Numbers that are doubles. The numbers 0, 2, 4, 6, 8, 10, etc., are even. The number 28 is even because it is 14 + 14.

F

Face (Unit 17)
A two-dimensional shape that is one side of a three-dimensional shape.

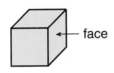

Fact Families (Unit 11)
Related math facts. These four number sentences are a fact family:
1 + 2 = 3
2 + 1 = 3
3 − 2 = 1
3 − 1 = 2

Flat (Unit 6)
A block that is one of the base-ten pieces. A flat is made of 100 bits. It often represents 100. (See also base-ten pieces.)

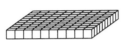

Flip (Unit 15)
A way of moving a two-dimensional shape. These dotted triangles are flipped over the lines.

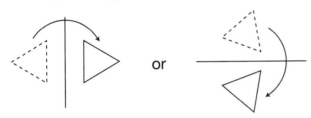

Function Machine (Unit 19)
A "machine" that follows a rule. It gives exactly one output number for any input number. This is a data table for an "Add 2" machine.

Input	Output
0	2
1	3
5	7
18	20

G

Gram (Unit 8)
The basic unit used to measure mass in the metric system. An ounce is about 28 grams. One gram is about the mass of a raisin.

H

Hand Span (Unit 4)
The distance from the tip of your thumb to the tip of your baby finger with your hand spread as wide as possible.

Horizontal Axis (Unit 2)
In a coordinate grid, the left/right axis.

I

Interval (Unit 2 & Unit 5)
All the numbers between (and including) two numbers.

J

K

L

Leftover (Unit 12 & Unit 19)
A number that remains or is left in a problem about equal sharing.

Line Symmetry (Unit 15)
A shape has line symmetry if it can be folded into two matching halves.

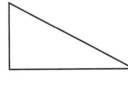
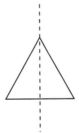

This shape has line symmetry. This shape does not have line symmetry.

Line of Symmetry (Unit 15)
A line through a shape. If you fold the shape along this line, then one half of the figure matches the other.

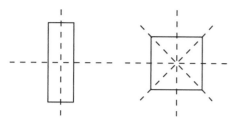

The dotted lines are lines of symmetry.

M

Mass (Unit 8 & Unit 10)
Mass is the amount of matter in an object. Metric units for mass are grams and kilograms. An object with a mass of one kilogram has a weight of about 2.2 pounds (on Earth). The mass of an object is the same everywhere, but its weight may vary. For example, if an object has a mass of 1 kilogram on Earth, it would have a mass of 1 kilogram on the moon, but it would weigh only one-sixth as much as it does on Earth.

Median (Unit 5)
The number "in the middle" of a set of data. Example: Jonah rolled a car down a ramp three times. The first time it rolled 30 cm. The second time it rolled 28 cm. The third time it rolled 33 cm. He put the numbers in order: 28 cm, 30 cm, 33 cm. 30 cm is the median because it is in the "middle" of his data.

Meniscus (Unit 10)
The curved surface formed when a liquid creeps up the side of a graduated cylinder.

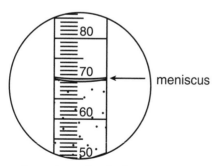

← meniscus

A graduated cylinder containing 69 cc.

Meter (Unit 5)
A unit of length in the metric system. A meter is a bit more that 39 inches.

Mr. Origin (also Ms. Origin) (Unit 18)
A plastic figure that helps children learn about direction and distance. Mr. Origin has a mitten on his right hand and a button on his front.

Multiplication Number Sentence (Unit 12)
A number sentence uses numbers and symbols instead of words to describe a problem. A multiplication number sentence describes a multiplication problem. For example, a multiplication number sentence for the problem "5 birds landed on a branch. Each bird had two seeds. How many seeds do all 5 birds have?" is $5 \times 2 = 10$.

N

Number Sentence (Unit 12)
A number sentence uses numbers and symbols instead of words to describe a problem. For example, a number sentence for the problem "5 birds landed on a branch. Two more birds also landed on the branch. How many birds are on the branch?" is $5 + 2 = 7$.

O

Odd Number (Unit 2)
A number that is not even. The odd numbers are 1, 3, 5, 7, 9, and so on.

P

Parallel Lines (Unit 15)
Lines that do not meet. Lines that are always the same distance apart.

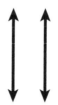

Perimeter (Unit 20)
The distance around a two-dimensional shape.

Place Value (Unit 6)
The value of a digit in a number. For example, the 5 is in the hundreds place in 4573, so it stands for 500.

Prism (Unit 17)
A type of 3-dimensional shape. Examples:

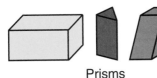

Prisms   Not a Prism

Pyramid (Unit 17)
A type of 3-dimensional shape. Examples:

Triangular pyramid   Rectangular pyramid

Q

R

Rectangle (Unit 15)
A shape with four sides and with four square corners.

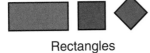

Rectangles   Not a
                        Rectangle

Rectangular Prism (Unit 17)
A prism whose faces are all rectangles.

Rectangular prism

Rectangular Pyramid (Unit 17)
A pyramid with a rectangle for a base.

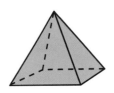

Rectangular pyramid

Reflection (Unit 15)
See flip.

Related Facts (Unit 11)
Fact families. For example, these facts are related:
$1 + 2 = 3$
$2 + 1 = 3$
$3 - 2 = 1$
$3 - 1 = 2$

Remainder (Unit 12)
A number that remains or is left after a division problem.

Rotation (Unit 15)
See turn.

Rotational Symmetry (Unit 15)
See turn symmetry.

S

Sample (Unit 13)
A smaller group taken out of a large collection.

Skinny (Unit 6)
A block that is one of the base-ten pieces. It is made of 10 bits. It often represents 10. (See also base-ten pieces.)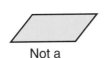

Slide (Unit 15)

A way of moving a two-dimensional shape. It moves a shape a certain distance in a certain direction.

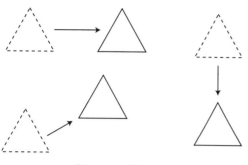

Sliding a triangle

Sphere (Unit 17)

A type of three-dimensional shape. A basketball is a common object shaped like a sphere.

Square (Unit 4 & Unit 15)

A rectangle that has four sides of equal length.

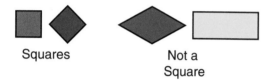

Squares   Not a Square

Square Centimeter (sq cm) (Unit 16)

The area of a square that is 1 cm long on each side.

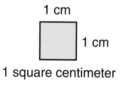

1 cm

1 cm

1 square centimeter

Standard Unit of Measure (Unit 5)

Universally accepted quantities used in measuring variables, e.g., centimeters and inches are standard units used to measure length and square centimeters and square inches are used to measure area.

Sum (Unit 3)

The answer to an addition problem.

Survey (Unit 19)

An investigation carried out by collecting data and then analyzing it.

T

Tally Marks (Unit 2)

A way to record a count by making marks. Tallies are usually grouped in fives, ||||| |||.

Translation (Unit 15)

See slide.

Trapezoid (Unit 15)

A four-sided shape with exactly one pair of parallel sides.

Trapezoids   Not Trapezoids

Triangular Prism (Unit 17)

A prism with a triangular base.

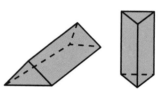

Triangular prisms

Triangular Pyramid (Unit 17)

A pyramid with a triangular base.

Triangular pyramid

Turn (Unit 15)

A way of moving a two-dimensional shape. A turn moves a shape around a point in its center.

Before   After

Triangle before and after half turn.

Turn Symmetry (Unit 15)
A shape has turn symmetry if you can turn it around a point in its center so that it "fits" itself. For example, a square has turn symmetry.

Two-dimensional Shapes (Unit 17)
Flat shapes.

Two-pan Balance (Unit 8)
A device for measuring mass that works by balancing an object against standard masses. Also called an equal-arm balance.

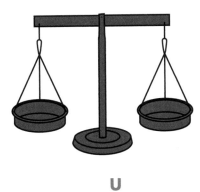

U

Unit (of Measurement) (Unit 10 & Unit 16)
A fixed amount used to measure. For example, centimeter, foot, kilogram, and quart are units of measurement.

V

Value (Unit 13)
The possible outcomes of a variable. For example, red, green, and blue are possible values for the variable *color*. Two meters and 6 inches are possible values for the variable *length*.

Variable (Unit 4 & Unit 13)
Something that changes or varies in an investigation.

Vertex (Unit 17)
See corner.

Volume (Unit 8, & Unit 10)
The measure of the amount of space occupied by an object. Volume is measured in cubic units.

W

Weight (Unit 6, Unit 7 & Unit 10)
Weight is a measure of the pull of gravity on an object. In the U.S. weight is usually measured in the English system that uses ounces and pounds as units of measure. If an object has a weight of 1 pound on Earth, it would have a weight of 1/6 pound on the moon, even though it would have the same mass as it does on Earth.

Width (of a rectangle) (Unit 16)
The distance along one side of a rectangle is the length and the distance along an adjacent side is the width.

X

Y

Z

Index

The index provides page references for the *Student Guide*. Definition or explanation of key terms can be found in the glossary. A good source for information on the location of topics in the curriculum is the *Scope and Sequence* in Section 5 of the *Teacher Implementation Guide*.

Edge, 509
Estimation
    addition, 217–218, 229, 237–240, 243–244
    counting, 67
    length, 55, 85–91, 107–114, 119–120
    measurement, 94
    subtraction, 293, 295

Face, shapes, 509, 511
Fractions, 365–375, 379–415, 579, 583–594
    addition, 379–383
    and area, 461–463
    area model, 379–391, 415
    paper folding and, 367–373
Function machine, 557–565, 581–582
Functions, 557–573

Games
    Add to 100, 232
    Cover Up, 43
    Difference War, 299
    Fraction Concentration, 413–414
    Fraction War, 413–414
    Monkey Treats, 323–325
    Moving on the 200 Chart, 27–29
    Not More Than 100, 139
    Take Your Places, Please, 151–155
    Spin and Add, 31–33
    Symmetry Game, 443
    What's My Rule?, 559
Geoboard, 591
    area on, 481–488
    puzzles, 485–488
Geometry riddles, 513
Graduated cylinder, reading volume, 236–281
Grouping and counting, 55, 65, 67, 83
Grouping and sharing, 313–314

Half-inch grid paper, 313–314
Halves, 441
Height, 70–74, 81–85
    measurement, 106
Hemisphere, 517

Input-output data table, 557–558, 565, 581–582
Interval, 94

King Gupta, 227

L

Labs *See* TIMS Laboratory Experiments
Length
    estimation, 55, 107–114, 119–120
    measurement, 70–74, 81–91, 94, 103–117
    of a rectangle, 469, 473

M

Maps, 525–545
  creating, 529–531
Mass, 194–211
  comparing and ordering objects, 194–195, 199
  measuring in grams, 203–211
Math facts strategies, 61
Measurement, 267–270
  arm span, 70–74
  centimeters, 103, 105–121
  distance, 114–117, 121
  estimation, 94
  height, 99, 106
  inches, 99, 576–578, 583
  length, 70–74, 81–87, 94, 103–121
  with links, 70–74, 81–87, 94
  meters, 109–111
  in meters and centimeters, 103–121
  prediction, 94
Median, 114
Meniscus, 259
Meter tape, 103
Money, 45, 289, 594
  addition, 31–33, 237–245
  animal trading cards, 5–9
  estimation, 215–217
  number sentences, 47, 332
  problem solving, 64, 225, 305–310
  word problems, 39–41
Mr. Origin, 520–525, 528, 535
Multiple trials, 114
Multiplication, 317–334
Multiplication and division, 313–327

N

Number line, 97–101
Number patterns, Gzorp, 567–573
Number sentences, 17–18, 20–23, 43, 47, 173–176, 181
  division, 319–320, 335–340
  money, 332
  multiplication, 323–325, 329–334
  problems, 341
  writing, 341

O

P

Pattern blocks, 437–447
  properties of shapes, 421
Patterns, identifying and extending, 567–573
Place value, 65, 67, 227
  ones, tens, and hundreds, 133–135
Place Value Mat, 133
Prediction, measurement, 94

Q

R

Rectanglar prism, 490, 509
Rectanglar pyramid, 490, 497, 509, 517

S

Scales
  graduated cylinders, 249–250, 255, 259
  reading and interpreting, 249–263
  speedometer, 252
  thermometers, 251
  two-pan balance, 194, 197, 199, 206–211
Shape riddles, 423
Shapes
  comparing, 167, 491, 505
  faces, 509, 511
  length and width, 470–474
  properties, 421–423
  3-dimensional, 490–517
  vertex, 509, 511
Sorting, 50–53, 57
Sorting and classifying, 344–354
  two-variable, 351–352
Sphere, 490, 517
Subtraction
  estimation, 293, 295
  facts, 285–287
  multidigit, 295–299
  problem solving, 291
Survey, family size, 548–553
Symmetry
  line, 437–445
  line of, 437–445
  turn, 437–439, 447